# THE NEW HOTEL

## INTERNATIONAL HOTEL AND RESORT DESIGN 3

MICHAEL KAPLAN

**HOTELS**
THE MAGAZINE OF THE WORLDWIDE HOTEL INDUSTRY

## FOREWORD BY ISADORE SHARP

**FOUR SEASONS ◆ REGENT HOTELS AND RESORTS**

Architecture & Interior Design Library

AN IMPRINT OF

PBC INTERNATIONAL, INC.

*Distributor to the book trade in the United States and Canada*
Rizzoli International Publications
through St. Martin's Press
175 Fifth Avenue
New York, NY 10010

*Distributor to the art trade in the United States and Canada*
PBC International, Inc.
One School Street
Glen Cove, NY 11542

*Distributor throughout the rest of the world*
Hearst Books International
1350 Avenue of the Americas
New York, NY 10019

Library of Congress Cataloging–in–Publication Data

Kaplan, Michael A.
    The new hotel: international hotel & resort design 3 / by Michael Kaplan and Hotels.
        p.    cm.
    Includes indexes.
    ISBN 0-86636-396-3 (HB : alk. paper). — ISBN 0-86636-490-0 (PB : alk. paper)
    1. Hotels. 2. Resort architecture. I. Hotels II. Title
NA7800.K33  1996                        95–52294
728'.5—dc20                             CIP

CAVEAT— Information in this text is believed accurate, and will pose no
problem for the student or casual reader. However, the author was often
constrained by information contained in signed release forms, information
that could have been in error or not included at all. Any misinformation
(or lack of information) is the result of failure in these attestations. The
author has done whatever is possible to insure accuracy.

*For Melodie DeWitt Kaplan*

Designed by Karin Martin

Color separation by AD.VER.srl, Italy
Printing and binding by Dai Nippon Printing Group

10 9 8 7 6 5 4 3 2 1

Printed in Hong Kong

# CONTENTS

# FOREWORD

WHAT DOES LUXURY MEAN TO TODAY'S TRAVELER? There was a time when "travel" and "luxury" together in one thought inspired visions of opulence. Lavishness. Extravagance. But these are words of the past. Luxury today is about comfort, functionality and personalized, unobtrusive service that anticipates guests' needs.

The French aviator and author Antoine de Saint-Exupéry once wrote, "In anything at all, perfection is finally attained not when there is no longer anything to add, but when there is no longer anything to take away." To the hospitality industry, this means every feature of a hotel or resort must enhance the travel experience in a meaningful way. There is no room for waste.

As a hotelier for more than 30 years, and an architect by training, I have made it my life's work to create hotels and resorts that provide travelers with luxury in the truest sense of the word. For most of those years, Christopher Wallis, executive vice president, has worked closely with me to realize this vision, overseeing every stage of design and construction of every hotel and resort we've developed. Today, our properties represent a diversity of locations; their common thread is their ability to meet the expectations of the global traveler.

The hotels and resorts in this book are all stellar examples of luxury in design. The hotelier in me admires the ingenious approaches each has taken to accommodate today's international traveler. The architect appreciates their masterful blend of beauty and function. I am sure that you will share my enthusiasm.

**ISADORE SHARP**
*Founder, Chairman and Chief Executive Officer*
Four Seasons ◆ Regent Hotels and Resorts

# PREFACE

AS A BUSINESS TRAVELLER FOR OVER 30 YEARS, including the last eight as the publisher of an international magazine for hotel executives, I have stayed in or visited a good share of the great hotels of the world. Yet every time I enter a new hotel I have the same feeling of anticipation and curiosity. I immediately check out every aspect of my room, and then I roam the hotel and examine all the public areas, including the lobby, exercise room, pool, bars, restaurants and shops. I will do this even if I'm just there overnight and can't possibly use these facilities. I'm not quite sure what I am looking for, but I really enjoy doing it and I always find something new that I have never seen before. I love the great hotels.

There must be lots of people like me. After the severe slump in the hotel business in the early 1990s, luxury hotels have come back stronger than any other category and have enjoyed record levels of hotel room occupancy.

This is the fifth book on hotel design that we have produced in collaboration with PBC International. The orientation of all our books has been toward quality design, but this is our first book to focus specifically on bringing together the new designs that will set the standards for the hotels of tomorrow.

Most of the credits in our book should justifiably go to the designers of these great hotels, but I should note that designers cannot express their design concepts without the direction, collaboration, and consent of a visionary client. It is people like Isadore Sharp of Four Seasons who have encouraged and challenged designers to raise new standards of excellence with each new hotel. We must thank Mr. Sharp and his counterparts at other luxury hotel companies for bringing new levels of enjoyment and satisfaction to today's global traveler.

**DONALD T. LOCK**
*Publisher*
HOTELS

# INTRODUCTION

*The New Hotel: International Hotel & Resort Design 3* takes you on a tour of the finest, most innovatively designed hotels in the world. As the first part of this title implies, the book centers around facilities that are creating a new paradigm for business and pleasure lodging. Technologically turned out and poshly accoutremented, they provide comfortable beds, computer access, and historical subtexts that often derive directly from the sites themselves. Whether located in Bali or Beverly Hills, the hotels share an urbane sophistication that goes beyond geographical boundaries. Whatever travelers desire, the new hotels are there to deliver the goods with a sense of panache and worldly ease. Herewith is a bit of wisdom on the evolution and growth of the New Hotel from Robert J. DiLeonardo, president of DiLeonardo International.

**INTERVIEW WITH ROBERT J. DILEONARDO** *by Michael Kaplan*

**MICHAEL KAPLAN:** *What are the cutting-edge trends for New Hotels?*

**ROBERT J. DILEONARDO:** First, you have to break it down into urban hotels for business travelers and resort hotels for vacationers. Over the next decade resort hotels will take on spa amenities. People are becoming increasingly conscious of wellness—and resorts are adding that on levels beyond exercise rooms. You'll see it in the food selection and in a big push toward eco-tourism when an explorable area surrounds a resort. Travelers are becoming increasingly aware of the quality of life we have on this planet, and it is impacting the ways in which we design resorts for them.

**MK:** *What about in terms of urban hotels?*

**RJD:** City hotels are becoming office incubators. They're places where people go to create business from their rooms. So they need more and more business amenities. I'm talking about things like full-size desks, regular business chairs, two-line telephones, and fax/modem capabilities. For a project that we did in Brazil, we even included credenzas and file cabinets.

**MK:** *How are the chain hotels being impacted by all of this?*

**RJD:** Plain and simple, you can't cookie cut a hotel anymore. Maybe you can do it in the lower tier market, but as soon as you get up to the higher end, the hotels have to be culturally sensitive to

Robert J. DiLeonardo, president of the Warwick, Rhode Island-based DiLeonardo International, has played a major role in the dynamic direction in which hotel design is currently moving. Having spent the last 25 years designing properties around the world, DiLeonardo has learned numerous lessons about what it takes to make ground-breaking hotels successful in aesthetic as well as financial terms.

their locations and the cultural experiences that exist around those locations. Then, within that context, you fulfill the need of the traveling public.

**MK:** *But didn't it used to be that if you went to, say, a Marriott in New York or Milan—*

**RJD:** They were the same. But that doesn't fly anymore. You need to remain culturally sensitive. The work we did on the Providence Westin Hotel is a good example of that. The entire design of that hotel came out of a New England atmosphere, from an architectural point of view and from what is familiar in New England. People come there for a New England experience, not for a Southern California interior.

**MK:** *What cultural changes have contributed to the New Hotel paradigm?*

**RJD:** The baby boomer generation moving up one notch. There are such masses of people with large amounts of disposable income who are getting older. They are accustomed to traveling for business, and now, when they travel for pleasure, they think about the quality of their life. Travelers have undoubtedly become more sophisticated. They know what they want, and it's our challenge, in this market-driven industry, to provide it.

**MK:** *Grand old hotels seem to be riding a crest of popularity right now.*

**RJD:** The old hotels are absolutely glorious and full of charm. If you're willing to put enough money back into the building—and most of the time, I would venture to say, it costs you more to do that than it would to build a new one—you get a property that is incomparable. It's like a vintage car that has been taken care of. Whether you personally like the great old hotels or not, you can instantly appreciate them. But in renovating them, architects face many challenges. Meeting the code issues is a major challenge because at the same time you have to keep the inherent charm.

**MK:** *In recent years, during the New Hotel boom, what impresses you the most about the industry?*

**RJD:** I'm impressed by operators who go in and put the right product in the right market. Some companies are just so fabulous at understanding the various markets. That is what blows me away.

# THE NEW

# CITY HOTEL

**LEFT:** The front lobby staircase is designed with elements that recall classic New England architecture. **BELOW LEFT:** Overstuffed sofas imbue the sitting room lobby with an inviting mood. **BELOW RIGHT:** The Westin Hotel looms over Providence, Rhode Island, with the grandeur of an instant landmark. **OPPOSITE:** Marble pillars and a commanding view encircle the front lobby.

# PROVIDENCE, RHODE ISLAND
# THE WESTIN HOTEL

The inherent challenge in designing The Westin Hotel arose as much from the property itself as from what surrounds it — a convention center and very little else in the way of world-class amenities. Hence, designers and architects involved with the project needed to create a facility that could serve as a cultural gathering place for local people while remaining appropriate and comfortable for conventioneers. That it all had to be done on a restrictive budget makes the lush and charming Westin all the more remarkable.

**HOTEL COMPANY**
THE WESTIN HOTEL

**ARCHITECT**
THE NICHOLS PARTNERSHIP

**INTERIOR DESIGNER**
DILEONARDO INTERNATIONAL

**PHOTOGRAPHER**
WARREN JAGGER

The designers created a traditionally luxurious, five-star hotel rich in brocade fabrics and outfitted with custom-made pieces created by local artists. Its 363 guest rooms are decorated in an old-world style, complete with Chippendale reproductions and black lacquered side tables. Trompe l'oeil details and faux painting

techniques allowed the designers to maintain the desired level of

elegance without exceeding their budget. Yet little is spared in the

way of ambience: A sitting area in the lobby, for instance, features

overstuffed, slipcovered sofas and chairs around a copper and

glass cocktail table overflowing with magazines. The lighting is

atmospherically dim and support columns are done in faux marble.

The Westin features two restaurants, one casual (The Cafe)

and the other formal (Agora), both serving continental cuisine. The

Cafe emotes the feeling of an outdoor eatery, while Agora (which

was singled out in Esquire magazine's 1995 regional restaurant

round-up) fulfills a more formal dictate. Dramatically draped in

fabric, the resulting dining room, like the hotel itself, is clubby and

cozy and not the least bit stuffy.

**OPPOSITE ABOVE:** Parquet flooring and fine-crafted woodwork distinguish the entryway to the hotel's acclaimed Agora restaurant. **OPPOSITE BELOW:** Formal but comfortable, the Agora features upholstered chairs, patterned carpeting, and softly draped fabric in pleasing autumnal tones. **ABOVE LEFT:** A barrel-vaulted ceiling adds drama while unifying the restaurant and bar areas. **ABOVE RIGHT:** Parquet floors and luxurious window treatments add to the atmosphere of casually elegant cocktailing. **LEFT:** French doors, fine paintings, and elegant chandeliers enhance the private dining room.

OPPOSITE TOP LEFT: Wainscoting and window treatments add traditional touches to a spacious meeting room. OPPOSITE TOP RIGHT: The beautifully appointed ballroom provides a perfect setting for elegant catered affairs. OPPOSITE BOTTOM LEFT: Chandeliers and fine art mark the way to the Westin's ballrooms and meeting facilities. OPPOSITE BOTTOM RIGHT: A jazzy theme runs through the hotel's more casual cocktail lounge. LEFT: Guest suites radiate upscale New England charm. BELOW: All rooms are decorated in a comfortably residential style.

THIS PAGE: The hotel's casual restaurant, The Cafe, with its garden-style furniture, offers a perfect spot for breakfast, lunch or dinner. The sky-scene mural, painted by a local artisan, helps to create a virtual alfresco dining experience.

OPPOSITE: Guests enjoy swimming and working out under natural light at the hotel's domed health club.

HOTEL COMPANY
MANILA DIAMOND HOTEL

ARCHITECT
K. HARA ASSOCIATED ARCHITECTS
AND ENGINEERS

INTERIOR DESIGNER
HIRSCH BEDNER ASSOCIATES

PHOTOGRAPHER
ROBERT MILLER

MANILA, PHILIPPINES
# MANILA DIAMOND HOTEL

**TOP:** The hotel's main lobby boasts a grand staircase that seems custom-designed for a grand entrance. **ABOVE:** The Manila Diamond reigns as its city's premier hotel. **OPPOSITE:** A lavish welcome to visitors is provided in the main lobby with its diamond grid pattern on mahogany walls.

As day turns to night, the view from the Manila Diamond Hotel makes it easy to forget that you are in the middle of an intense city. Viewed across Manila Bay, sunsets are nothing short of inspirational, and that was part of what led to a hotel being built on this spot, right in the center of Manila. Community leaders hope that the Manila Diamond will contribute to reviving the old city.

A contemporary, 22-story high-rise, the Manila Diamond has 507 rooms and can be best described as an urban resort with state-of-the-art health club and spa. The hotel attracts international tourists, large numbers of Japanese businessmen, and many local people who are drawn to its convention facilities. Lavishly furnished, mahogany-paneled guest rooms all have high ceilings, crown molding, and black marble in the bathrooms. The Manila Diamond's ultracontemporary edge has been softened by natural motifs — including sun and moon, waves and earth, night and day — that have been incorporated into the hotel's interior design.

Though there are four restaurants located on the hotel's premises, The Bellevue truly stands out for its cuisine and its luxurious decor details: French limestone walls, parquet floors, and a domed ceiling painted with clouds.

**ABOVE:** Luxurious interiors and a sky-high view of the city are two assets of this suite's ultraluxe bathroom. **RIGHT:** The Manila Diamond's health spa is a state-of-the-art facility, designed in a classically rich manner. **OPPOSITE:** Rooms are cleanly and simply designed, with four-poster beds and custom-made furniture that has been produced by local manufacturers.

OPPOSITE: The addition of a waterfall adds a romantic touch to the hotel's inviting swimming pool. LEFT: The Sky Lounge is an ultracontemporary bar that's topped by a fiber-optic ceiling and features glass doors sandblasted with a sun and moon motif. BELOW: Modern and elegant, the hotel's three-meal restaurant is dominated by a dramatic fountain at its center.

**HOTEL COMPANY**
HYATT HOTELS INTERNATIONAL

**ARCHITECT**
OBAYASHI CORPORATION
DESIGN STUDIO #1

**INTERIOR DESIGNER**
WILSON & ASSOCIATES

**PHOTOGRAPHER**
JAIME ARDILES-ARCE

OSAKA, JAPAN
# HYATT REGENCY OSAKA

Business traveling is hard work. With that in mind, the Hyatt Regency Osaka strives to provide its executive clientele with comfort at the day's conclusion. The hotel's interior has been created by fusing traditional Japanese design philosophies with the features that international travelers require. The result is a facility that emotes tranquility, simplicity, and harmony while offering an exercise facility, 15 meeting rooms, a concierge club, and all the high-tech amenities that business travel currently demands.

The 500-room hotel is crowned by a rooftop pool and garden, where relaxation-inducing vistas meet the potential for stress-burning exercise. Japanese and water gardens dominate the ground floor, and a 27th-floor sky lounge offers magnificent views over Osaka Bay. Occupying a narrow site that is situated between office buildings and a convention hall, the Hyatt Regency Osaka is outfitted with furniture that has been scaled to Japanese standards. Besides fitting in with the local aesthetic, the strategy works particularly well since everything in the hotel is sleek, natural looking, and evocative of the Zen-like simplicity that plays such an integral role in classic Eastern design.

**OPPOSITE ABOVE:** Richly toned wood and marble enhance the hotel's check-in area. **OPPOSITE BELOW:** The hotel's facade reveals Eastern and Western architectural elements. **ABOVE:** A grand marble staircase surrounds a dramatic sculpture by a local artist. **LEFT:** Contemporary art is tastefully installed throughout the hotel.

**TOP:** Located on the roof, the indoor pool is cleanly designed and coolly inviting. **CENTER:** Chairs near the rooftop pool look out onto Osaka's growing Technoport area. **BOTTOM:** Guest room furnishings are scaled to Japanese standards.

**ALL BELOW:** A modern aesthetic is at the core of all guest room furnishings. Muted colors provide a tranquil, relaxing ambience, while bathrooms are mirrored, sleek and modern.

ABOVE LEFT: Crystal, orchids, and fine linen are exquisite details in the shimmering Crystal Ballroom. ABOVE RIGHT: The Cafe provides a pleasant spot for casual dining. RIGHT: Contemporary furnishings complement the architecture in the lounge.

**LEFT:** The entrance to Ten Kuh reflects tasteful simplicity. **BELOW:** Architectural elements and table settings provide an effective backdrop for Ten Kuh's renowned Chinese cuisine.

# FOUR SEASONS HOTEL NEW YORK

As soon as you wake up in Manhattan's I.M. Pei-designed Four

Seasons Hotel, you will realize that you are in a modern facility

where your needs were considered before you had a chance to

consider them yourself. Behind each bed is a button that allows

you to open and close the room's drapes, thus allowing morning

light to flow into your room before your toes touch the carpet.

Other appealing touches include black-out curtains over the

openable windows, visual fire alarms for hearing-impaired guests,

and "do not disturb" buttons located near the bed. Everything in

the hotel seems to have been created with the guests' collective

comfort in mind.

The 387-room hotel has been designed and constructed in an

**HOTEL COMPANY**
Four Seasons & Regent Hotels

**ARCHITECTS**
Pei Cobb Freed and Partners
Frank Williams & Associates

**INTERIOR DESIGNER**
Chhada, Siembieda & Partners

**PHOTOGRAPHER**
Peter Vitale

**OPPOSITE LEFT:** The hotel's architecture is replete with design references to the 1920s and '30s. **OPPOSITE RIGHT:** Columned entrances lead to raised-level lobbies. **TOP & LEFT:** Meeting suites for focused business sessions contain individual workstations. **ABOVE:** Fifty Seven Fifty Seven Bar inhabits a bold, contemporary space.

ultracontemporary manner, though it's loaded with historical references to the 1920s and '30s. The building's exterior and interior walls, for example, are clad in Magny limestone from France, the same material that had been used in the Louvre expansion; it creates an overall impression of great volume and height for a massive lobby that occupies the hotel's entire depth between two blocks. Catering primarily to business travelers, each of the Four Seasons' rooms — which average a comfortable 600 square feet, but run as large as 3,000 square feet — comes equipped with a fax machine, private numbers that are available on request, two dual-line telephones with personal computer outlets, and an oval partners-style desk alongside two leather-upholstered chairs. Bathrooms are of Florentine marble, tubs fill up in 60 seconds, and glass-enclosed showers have pressure-balancing thermostat-controlled fixtures.

The hotel houses a bistro-style restaurant, elegant bar, and relaxed lobby lounge. There are well-equipped business and fitness centers as well as secretarial and interpreting services. A menu of messages — customized to aid everything from shopping sprees to business presentations — is made available to guests.

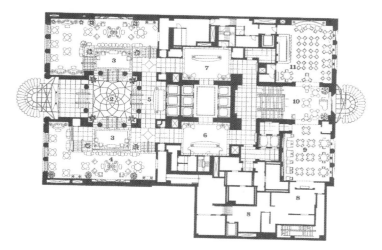

OPPOSITE ABOVE: The bath-room walls and floor are covered in Florentine marble. OPPOSITE BELOW: Rooms and suites come equipped with electronic controls so that drapes can be opened and closed while guests remain in bed. LEFT ABOVE: The Presidential Suite's living room has the look of an elegant Manhattan apartment. LEFT BELOW: Guest room sizes begin at a luxurious 600 square feet. ABOVE: Dressing areas feature ample storage, a wall safe, and enor-mous mirrors.

# HOTEL INTER-CONTINENTAL LOS ANGELES

LOS ANGELES, CALIFORNIA

**HOTEL COMPANY**
INTER-CONTINENTAL

**ARCHITECT**
FLATOW, MOORE, BRYAN,
SHAFFER & MCCABE

**INTERIOR DESIGNER**
DESIGN CONTINUUM, INC.

**PHOTOGRAPHY**
COURTESY OF HOTEL
INTER-CONTINENTAL LOS ANGELES

Though downtown Los Angeles lacks the showbiz cachet of Beverly Hills, it nevertheless qualifies as the city's unrivaled business center. The first downtown hotel to be built in over a decade, the Inter-Continental has been designed in a neoclassical style, influenced by California-casual aesthetics and infused with Asian overtones. Following a healthy-body/healthy-mind philosophy, the hotel houses top-notch workout facilities as well as two highly regarded restaurants — both with stunning views.

Built atop prestigious Bunker Hill, where California's most upscale families owned mansions in the 1920s, the 433-room hotel manages to be simultaneously comfortable and elegant. Its corporate guests take advantage of meeting and banquet facilities that are spread out across 20,000 square feet of space and topped off by the hotel's grand ballroom; additionally, the outdoor Watercourt is available for receptions of up to 4,500 people. For in-room activities, hotel guests can rent personal computers, printers, and VCRs directly from the concierge's desk. Operating as an

OPPOSITE ABOVE: The hotel's facade is a recent downtown landmark. OPPOSITE BELOW: The Boardroom provides a no-nonsense setting for small-scale meetings. ABOVE: Contemporary art adds a sense of grandeur to the hotel's lobby. LEFT: The ballroom has multi-media capabilities for meetings and presentations, as well as an elegant ambience for catered events.

office away from the office, the Inter-Continental offers access to a

wide range of business services and equipment: secretaries,

translators, presentation aids, massive-mailing capabilities, and the

rental of communication devices that range from beepers to

cellular telephones to walkie-talkies. Guest rooms — designed in

compliance with the Americans With Disabilities Act — all come

with two dual-line telephones, multi-lingual remote-access voice

mail, oversized desks, and fax/modem capabilities.

OPPOSITE ABOVE: The Presidential Suite's amenities include a baby grand piano. OPPOSITE BELOW: All guest rooms include fax/modem capabilities. LEFT: The Watercourt can accommodate as many as 4,500 people. ABOVE: An artist's rendering captures the casual elegance of the Watercourt.

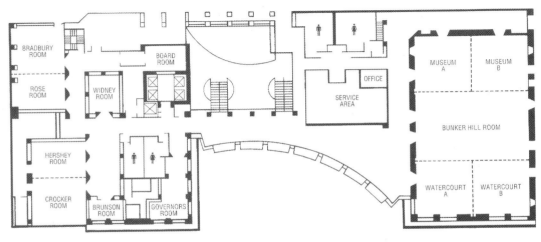

# SYDNEY, AUSTRALIA
# PARK HYATT SYDNEY

It is said that you should live as well on the road as you do at home. Few visitors to the Park Hyatt in Sydney, Australia, will have to contend with that dilemma. A jewel of a hotel, located in the city's historic Rocks district, it offers butler service in all guest rooms and exudes clubby luxury. Considering that it is Sydney's only hotel with such a desirable location and such elegant accommodations, it is no wonder that the Park Hyatt Sydney is a favored stop on the itineraries of traveling celebrities and business executives.

**HOTEL COMPANY**
HYATT HOTELS INTERNATIONAL

**ARCHITECT**
ANCHOR MORTLOCK
& WOOLLEY PTY., LTD.

**INTERIOR DESIGNER**
HIRSCH BEDNER ASSOCIATES

**PHOTOGRAPHER**
JAIME ARDILES-ARCE

Unlike some hotels, which position themselves to welcome locals as well as travelers, the Park Hyatt Sydney strives to maintain an air of exclusivity. The 157-room hotel, laden with Australian art, is there exclusively for its guests. Hence, there are no function rooms, only a small — but beautifully turned out — business center, and a health club facility that is closed to outsiders.

OPPOSITE ABOVE: Subtle lighting and a curved entryway set a welcoming tone. OPPOSITE BELOW: The elegant business center provides a clubby ambience for meetings. ABOVE: Waterfront views abound at the Hotel's restaurants. LEFT: Located in a historic district, the hotel had to adhere to strictly-enforced design guidelines.

The hotel is built on Sydney's waterfront, which is great for views but bad for noise from the nearby harbor bridge. To alleviate that, the design/architecture team decided to double-glaze rooms and planned construction so that most quarters would be situated away from that side of the harbor. All rooms are large, outfitted with walk-in closets and elegant bathrooms; most rooms have waterfront views that can be enjoyed from individual balconies. Besides its guest rooms, the Park Hyatt Sydney boasts outdoor suites, which are so popular with guests that Billy Joel and Frank Sinatra recently locked horns in a headline-making altercation over who would get the last remaining one.

OPPOSITE ABOVE: Most guest rooms feature terraces and harbor views. OPPOSITE BELOW: The hotel's formal dining room features a fine wine cellar and modern Australian cuisine. ABOVE: An additional suite was recently added to accommodate the demand of upscale guests. LEFT: Separate dressing tables are featured in all of the hotel's guest rooms. BELOW LEFT: Large and elegant, the wood- and marble-accented bathrooms invite luxuriating soaks in the tub.

# THE ROYAL ABJAR HOTEL

Building a hotel in a heavily Islamic, Middle Eastern city can be a daunting task. While adhering to local cultural and religious standards, the facility also needs to hold appeal for upscale international business people. The Royal Abjar manages to do that — as can be evidenced by its popularity among travelers as well as the wealthy locals who rent its function rooms for weddings — by imbuing Western design sensibilities with a feel for the Islamic way of life.

Built between 1987 and 1992 with a $69-million design budget, the 281-room five-star hotel has been configured in a sleek European style. There are also touches that are clearly Arabic in origin: camel motifs in the coffee shop, fabric-draped ceilings, and room dividers that recall the entryways to a sheik's private quarters. Guest rooms are comfortable and spacious, Western in design, and furnished primarily with softly colored wooden pieces. The atrium lobby has a soaring ceiling adorned with fly bridges that cross at different levels and are intersected by a pair of mobile sculptures. Seven restaurants serve a wide range of cuisines that include local delicacies, Italian food, and Asian pastries.

**ABOVE LEFT:** A swimming pool and jacuzzi provide a respite from Dubai's arid climate. **ABOVE RIGHT:** Fit for a potentate, the hotel lobby is sprawling, modern, and elegant. **RIGHT:** Arabic design elements have been infused with Western libations.

**HOTEL COMPANY**
THE ROYAL ABJAR HOTEL

**ARCHITECT**
THE FRASER NAG PARTNERS

**INTERIOR DESIGNER**
DiLEONARDO INTERNATIONAL

**PHOTOGRAPHER**
ROBERT MILLER

**ABOVE:** Ceiling mobiles serve as striking design elements throughout the hotel. **RIGHT:** Guest rooms have all been configured with a sleek, Western sensibility in mind.
**BELOW:** A fitting motif dominates the Camel Coffee Shop's buffet.

**HOTEL COMPANY**
FOUR SEASONS & REGENT HOTELS

**ARCHITECT**
SAA PARTNERSHIP

**INTERIOR DESIGNER**
HIRSCH BEDNER ASSOCIATES

**PHOTOGRAPHER**
ROBERT MILLER

# SINGAPORE
# FOUR SEASONS HOTEL SINGAPORE

Located in one of the world's most intensely business-oriented cities, the Four Seasons Singapore strikes a neat balance between fulfilling its guests' professional needs while providing them with leisurely ways to unwind. The hotel features indoor and rooftop swimming pools, a full health club complete with sports medicine clinic, air-conditioned tennis courts, and four meeting rooms. Built on a residential scale, the Four Seasons has been designed so that a series of rooms flows from its entrance to the reception area and restaurants. Its layout is based on the great houses of 18th-century England, designed by Inigo Jones and the Adam brothers.

Attracting a mix of business and vacation travelers, the 257-room hotel is attached to a shopping galleria, affords direct access to Singapore's main shopping street, and is convenient to the city's underground railway system. Rooms are designed and decorated in a plush European style, and all are appointed with multi-disc players, safes, voice mail, and fax/modem capabilities. Particularly elegant are the hotel's marbled bathrooms with their separate showers, water closets, deep bathtubs, and bidets. Fitting for a city as international as Singapore, its Four Seasons features five food and beverage outlets with cuisines that range from Californian to Italian to Cantonese.

OPPOSITE ABOVE: Visitors to the health club's lounge enjoy post-workout drinks and meals from the buffet. OPPOSITE LEFT: Lushly landscaped, the rooftop pool encourages guests to forget that they are in the middle of a bustling Asian city. TOP LEFT: Guests are serenaded as they enjoy dinner in an elegant setting. TOP RIGHT: Spacious bathrooms at the Four Seasons Singapore sport double vanities and deep soaking bathtubs. ABOVE LEFT: The Patio Cafe is a fine dining room located on the hotel's ground floor. ABOVE RIGHT: Suites are designed with a mix of Singaporean and European elements.

**HOTEL COMPANY**
SOFITEL

**ARCHITECT**
PROJECT BUCHARESTI
IN COLLABORATION WITH BOUYGUES

**INTERIOR DESIGNER**
INTER ART ETUDES

**PHOTOGRAPHER**
ALAIN GOUSTARD

BUCHAREST, ROMANIA

# HOTEL SOFITEL BUCHAREST

Located in a city where nearly all edifices are ancient, the Hotel Sofitel Bucharest stands out as a beacon toward the 21st century. The hotel's courting of an international clientele of business travelers can be evidenced by the flags of many nations near its circular driveway and the facility's close proximity to Bucharest's airport. Located five minutes from the city's business district, the Sofitel also serves as headquarters for The World Trade Center where a great deal of Romanian-based business deals are consummated.

Local art adorns the walls of this contemporary 250-room hotel. The paintings are dramatic and heartfelt, with the kinds of bold colors and strong graphics that are not normally associated with Eastern Europe. The images decorate some guest rooms, which are designed in a spare, uncluttered but homey style. Meetings can be held in either an auditorium or ballroom, both of which offer modern audio/video capabilities. The furnishings for the hotel's bar had been inspired by elements from the 1930s, while the restaurant emotes a classical tone that's brought out by ancient bronze pieces recalling Bucharest's rich and fabled past.

OPPOSITE ABOVE: Hotel Sofitel Bucharest is a modern building in an ancient city. OPPOSITE BELOW: Marble floors and soaring columns lend a regal air to the hotel lobby. ABOVE: Paintings by contemporary Romanian artists enrich the hotel's decor. LEFT: Marble-accented bathrooms offer double-basin sinks and terry cloth robes. RIGHT: The hotel's auditorium comes equipped with audio/video capabilities.

**HOTEL COMPANY**
RENAISSANCE HOTELS

**ARCHITECTS**
THOMPSON VENTULETT STAINBACH &
ASSOCIATES, INC.
CARL TRIMBLE ARCHITECTS

**INTERIOR DESIGNER**
DILEONARDO INTERNATIONAL

**PHOTOGRAPHER**
JAIME ARDILES-ARCE

ATLANTA, GEORGIA
# STOUFFER CONCOURSE HOTEL

With the Stouffer Hotel located inside Atlanta's Hartsfield International Airport, layovers and canceled flights come to resemble rather pleasant inconveniences. Though airports and their surroundings traditionally function as doorways to and from somewhere else, rather than destinations in their own right, the Stouffer emotes a strong sense of place. It is pure, upmarket Atlanta, decorated in a style that its designer, DiLeonardo International, defines as "New Southern." The look is characterized by dark woods, oversized spaces, and gold detailing on lamps, picture frames, and desks.

Though the five-star hotel boasts 400 rooms, many of its best customers never spend a night there. Due to the Stouffer's location, it serves as a convenient spot for local business people who need to meet with out-of-towners. The hotel offers extensive meeting rooms as well as a bar and restaurant, the latter operating as a three-meal-a-day buffet.

Hanging plants and a grand piano imbue the atrium with an air of Southern elegance, providing the final touch to a facility that transcends the typical expectation of an airport hotel.

**OPPOSITE ABOVE:** Formal meals can be easily arranged through the hotel's catering department.
**OPPOSITE BELOW:** Lobbies are warm and inviting, creating the illusion that you are in the heart of a sophisticated, downtown area — not adjacent to the airport. **ABOVE:** Guest rooms are furnished in a style that the hotel's designers characterize as "New Southern."
**LEFT:** Four-hundred rooms look down on the Stouffer's attractive atrium.

HOTEL COMPANY
RIHGA INTERNATIONAL

ARCHITECT
FRANK WILLIAMS & ASSOCIATES

INTERIOR DESIGNER
BIRCH COFFEY DESIGN ASSOCIATES

PHOTOGRAPHER
PETER PAIGE & ASSOCIATES

NEW YORK, NEW YORK

# RIHGA ROYAL HOTEL NEW YORK

One of the tallest hotels in New York City, the RIHGA has been designed to recall skyscrapers from the 1920s and '30s. This is evident in the building's ultra-elegant lobby and corridors, where black lacquer console tables support lamps with gold-leaf bases. However, a very '90s design rears itself in the hotel's hallways: They have been designed without recesses so as to offer an open line of sight for security purposes.

The 500-suite RIHGA caters primarily to business travelers. Its horizontal bay windows create a set-back effect, offering panoramic views of the Manhattan skyline and East River. Room furnishings are all contemporary, subdued, and comfortable; this is especially true of the three Hospitality Suites, which measure 2,500 square feet, feature expansive living rooms, three separate sitting areas, large marble bars, and separate bedrooms. All rooms feature three dual-line telephones, computer and fax outlets, individual room safes, computerized message retrieval, and checkout via television. Catering to its corporate clientele, the hotel features an extensive business center, health club, 24-hour in-suite dining, and a complimentary shuttle to Wall Street.

**OPPOSITE TOP:** Modeled after a 1930s skyscraper, the RIHGA ranks among the tallest buildings in Manhattan. **OPPOSITE ABOVE:** The opulent lobby has been inspired by Park Avenue residential entryways built in the 1920s and '30s.

**OPPOSITE BELOW:** The sleekly designed Halcyon Lounge offers a sense of bygone elegance. **TOP LEFT:** All suites feature marble bathrooms, with glass-enclosed showers and bathtubs. **TOP RIGHT:** Guest rooms are decorated in a comfortable, contemporary style. **ABOVE:** Upper floor suites offer fax machines, cellular telephones, and private phone lines. **LEFT:** A brass chandelier greets visitors at the entrance of the Halcyon Restaurant.

# HYATT REGENCY ISTANBUL

Building a new hotel in an ancient city represents a formidable

challenge: Making it modern without making it alien to its

surroundings. Designers and architects who were behind the Hyatt

Regency Istanbul accomplished this by infusing the hotel with all of

the modern amenities that international travelers expect, while

accenting it with details that are redolent of old-world Istanbul.

Attracting a mix of business travelers and tourists, the 369-

room hotel features five meeting rooms, a ballroom, a casino, and a

health club. Fitting for any hotel in Turkey, the Hyatt Regency

Istanbul provides a luxurious steam bath where visitors can unwind

from days of touring or deal making. Additionally, for guests who

like to keep in shape, the hotel boasts a lushly landscaped

swimming pool, workout facility, and juice bar. Following its design

**HOTEL COMPANY**
HYATT HOTELS INTERNATIONAL

**ARCHITECT**
WEIDELPLAN

**INTERIOR DESIGNER**
HIRSCH BEDNER ASSOCIATES

**PHOTOGRAPHER**
JAIME ARDILES-ARCE

**OPPOSITE:** Fired torches illuminate the deck around the Hyatt's swimming pool. **TOP:** Three meals are available daily at the more casual restaurant, Agora. **ABOVE:** The lobby lounge offers a great view of the hotel's beautifully adorned entrance. **LEFT:** Marble floors and a glittering chandelier add a touch of elegance to each guest's arrival.

**TOP:** Harry's Jazz Bar provides American music in a setting with Turkish underpinnings. **CENTER:** Turkish art has been employed in the decoration of the Hyatt Regency Istanbul's guest rooms. **BOTTOM:** A luxurious Turkish bath is part of the Istanbul experience. **OPPOSITE:** An open kitchen is part of the fine dining experience at the hotel's signature restaurant, Spasso.

strategy of combining modern hotel decor with classic Ottoman

touches, the Hyatt Regency Istanbul's rooms are decorated with

beautiful throw pillows, traditional Turkish rug designs, and locally

produced art. The hotel has two restaurants, a bar, and a nightclub

called Harry's Jazz Bar. While decidedly non-Turkish in music, the

club features Ottoman underpinnings in its decor.

# THE NEW

# RESORT HOTEL

# SANTA MONICA, CALIFORNIA
# SHUTTERS ON THE BEACH

HOTEL COMPANY
SHUTTERS ON THE BEACH

ARCHITECT
HILL ARCHITECTS

INTERIOR DESIGNER,
RESTAURANTS AND BAR
PAUL DRAPER AND ASSOCIATES

INTERIOR DESIGNER, GUEST
ROOMS AND PUBLIC SPACES
INTRADESIGN

PHOTOGRAPHER
MICHAEL WILSON PHOTOGRAPHY

The soul of Shutters on the Beach can be found in its bathrooms. Situated above nearly each bathtub is a window that avails a view of Santa Monica's beachfront. Due to the windows' strategic positioning, guests can sit in their tubs and look out at the ocean. This is a terrific metaphor for a hotel that aims to create a sense of fantasy while seamlessly blending in with its surroundings.

Attracting large numbers of film and media people, the 200-room hotel houses a grand ballroom and several function rooms. It is built in a three-story, "low rise" style that affords stunning ocean views and architecturally suggests a beachfront bungalow look that is quite popular in Southern California. In keeping with the hotel's beachy feel, open-air corridors are scattered throughout, and room furnishings are cool and unpretentious. Designed on a residential scale so that it feels more like a weekend home than a hotel, Shutters exudes warmth and intimacy. Its guest quarters, cleanly

**ABOVE:** Outdoor diners are afforded a view of Santa Monica Beach. **LEFT:** Extensive landscaping enriches the property while integrating it into its natural site. **OPPOSITE:** The pool area features an outdoor fireplace and a bar.

designed and decorated with light-colored furnishings, feature

fireplaces, double jacuzzi tubs, and "splash" radios that can be

taken to the beach; beach bags and umbrellas are also provided on

request. Accommodating business travelers, the hotel offers a wide

range of professional services including computer rentals, fax

machines, and secretarial assistance.

No luxury hotel in Los Angeles is complete without a well-

regarded restaurant. Shutters has two, both designed in an open,

airy, casual style. The hotel's more formal eatery, One Pico, ranks

among the best places on the West Coast for watching a sunset,

and each evening it fills with a mix of locals and tourists who stare

across the Pacific as they dine on grilled fish.

**OPPOSITE:** Decorated with natural materials and accessorized with seashells, public spaces are designed to resemble private living rooms.

**ABOVE:** The unpretentious accommodations are laid out to recall guest rooms in a private beach house.

**LEFT:** Many of the guest rooms come with working fireplaces.

**ABOVE LEFT:** The bar was designed to make guests in beach-wear feel comfortable without alienating more formally dressed patrons.

**ABOVE RIGHT:** The hotel's informal restaurant is best described as a California bistro — complete with a working display kitchen and modern Italian chairs. **RIGHT:** Casual elegance creates inviting ambience in the formal restaurant, One Pico.

**OPPOSITE:** Exposed beams and well-designed furnishings suggest a hand-crafted look.

**HOTEL COMPANY**
HYATT HOTELS INTERNATIONAL

**ARCHITECT**
HOK INTERNATIONAL ASIA PACIFIC LTD.

**INTERIOR DESIGNER**
HIRSCH BEDNER ASSOCIATES

**PHOTOGRAPHER**
JAIME ARDILES-ARCE

JAKARTA, INDONESIA
# GRAND HYATT JAKARTA

Indonesia is rich in history, architecture, and style. The people behind Grand Hyatt Jakarta designed this hotel to resemble a private Indonesian mansion rather than an international hotel. At the same time, though, they also realized that certain Western hotel conventions are necessary in order to make visitors feel comfortable. Their solution is an appealing compromise: European-style furniture and architecture augmented by Indonesian art, antiques, fabrics, and decor. The result is a hotel that truly features the best of both worlds.

The five-star luxury hotel attracts a combination of business and vacation travelers, though it also serves as a meeting place for locals who are entertaining. Convenient to Jakarta's most upmarket shopping mall and reigning as the city's first grand hotel, the Hyatt's amenities — grand ballroom, full business center, resort deck and health club, tennis courts, lavish suites, and regency club rooms —

OPPOSITE ABOVE: At night the Grand Hyatt shimmers as the finest hotel in Jakarta. OPPOSITE BELOW: The hotel lobby's marble floor was produced by Indonesian craftsmen, employing the local three-color palette. ABOVE: Viewed from above, the hotel atrium is a lavishly inviting space with grand staircases, fountains, and a jungle's worth of plant life. LEFT: Floral arrangements add a native touch to the Grand Hyatt's interior.

are unrivaled. Local craftsmen created much of the hotel's marble and its 411 rooms are elegantly turned out to luxury European standards, complete with canopied beds, beautifully carved armoires, and native art pieces.

Six restaurants are situated throughout the hotel, including a tea lounge, an elegant Chinese restaurant, and a farm-style Japanese eatery. For homesick Americans there is O'Reilley's bar, a faithful recreation of an upscale U.S.-style tavern. It's a fitting place in which to toast the hotel's magnificent melding of cultures.

OPPOSITE: Excellent workout facilities at the Grand Hyatt help define it as a world-class international hotel. **ABOVE:** Spacious suites and a large wine list make entertaining at the Grand Hyatt a pleasure. **LEFT:** Suites are furnished in a European style but accented with Indonesian touches.

RIGHT: The tea lounge provides a quiet, traditional respite for visitors to Indonesia. BELOW: Live music can be heard at the hotel's American-inspired bar. OPPOSITE: Following a swim in the Grand Hyatt Jakarta's pool, guests can enjoy seafood meals at the outdoor cafe.

LEFT: Natural light and plants brighten this upper lobby. BELOW: In the ground floor's main reception area, staff members give each guest a personalized welcome. OPPOSITE: As can be gleaned from this view of the lobby, art plays a major role in the design of the hotel. A budget of $1.5 million was put aside for the acquisition of contemporary works.

YOKOHAMA, JAPAN

# ROYAL PARK HOTEL NIKKO

Aptly located in the Minato Mirai 21, which translates to mean "future port for the 21st century," the Royal Park Hotel Nikko is truly a facility for the coming millennium. High-tech in every sense of the word, its guest rooms feature soundproof doors, electronic "do not disturb" signs, and in-room answering machines. Rooms on the higher-priced executive floors are outfitted with fax machines and provide breathtaking views. The last feature is particularly impressive when you consider that the five-star, 603-room hotel occupies the top 21 floors of the tallest building in Japan. Its elevators are among the fastest in the world.

The hotel attracts leisure travelers as well as convention trade and executives conducting business in Yokohama and/or nearby Tokyo. A major draw of the Nikko is its top-flight French

**HOTEL COMPANY**
NIKKO HOTELS INTERNATIONAL

**ARCHITECT**
STUBBINS ASSOCIATES

**INTERIOR DESIGNER**
WILSON & ASSOCIATES

**PHOTOGRAPHER**
ROBERT MILLER

restaurant, Le Ciel. Intentionally designed on a small scale, the restaurant offers no bad tables and is so busy that weekend dinner reservations need to be made a month in advance. The hotel also boasts a private dining room, Chinese and Japanese restaurants, a formal tea room, banquet halls, grand ballroom, and a 70th-floor skylounge where a breakfast buffet is offered.

A two-story lobby with a grand staircase introduces an East-meets-West design aesthetic that is maintained throughout the entire hotel.

OPPOSITE: Spectacular views of Yokohama augment the elegance of Le Ciel, the Royal Park Hotel Nikko's top restaurant. ABOVE: A gilded lattice pattern embellishes the ceiling cove at the entry to Le Ciel. ABOVE LEFT: At 441 square feet, the guest rooms are oversized by Japanese standards. LEFT: Bathrooms are luxurious with windows and marble walls.

# HYATT REGENCY KAUAI
### ISLAND OF KAUAI, HAWAII

Old Hawaii is alive and well within the walls of the Hyatt Regency Kauai. The 600-room $220-million hotel is comprised of several small buildings topped with steep, terra-cotta roofs and elegantly detailed inside with marble floors and inlays. Situated along the Pacific Ocean, the property has been built with lush gardens and man-made lagoons as its dominant theme. The combination of classic Hawaiian architecture merged with colorfully landscaped grounds — where fragile endemic flowers have been planted and special sprinkler systems have been installed — results in a virtual fantasy experience for a combination of business and pleasure travelers. Guests can imagine that they are wandering through a small, naturally beautiful community in a simpler Hawaii that has not yet become a haven for highrises and condos.

However, there is nothing simple about the Hyatt Regency's amenities and services. Major facilities there include 65,000 square

**HOTEL COMPANY**
HYATT HOTELS CORPORATION

**ARCHITECT**
WIMBERLY ALLISON TONG & GOO

**INTERIOR DESIGNER**
HIRSCH BEDNER ASSOCIATES

**PHOTOGRAPHERS**
OLIVIER KONING,
HOWARD J. WOLFF, DANA EDMONDS,
AND MILROY & MCALEER

**ABOVE:** Islands, palm trees and local foliage create the appearance of a tropical paradise. **RIGHT:** Traditional Hawaiian architecture and expansive outdoor spaces contribute to the Hyatt's elegance.

**ABOVE LEFT:** Lush landscaping and expansive ocean views abound at the Hyatt Regency Kauai. **ABOVE:** Regal black swans and colorful Koi add beauty and interest to the hotel's waterscape. **LEFT:** Artful lighting and a beamed ceiling cove create an inviting ambience in the lobby.

feet of banquet and meeting space, health and fitness spas that sprawl across 25,000 square feet, four tennis courts, and an 18-hole Robert Trent Jones II championship golf course. Additionally, the hotel boasts five lounges and restaurants, serving cuisine that ranges from platters of locally caught fish at Tidepools to ossubuco alla Milanese at a Northern Italian eatery called Dondero's. Though the property's amenity-rich rooms are large and well appointed, to stay inside is to miss the point, and the Hyatt Regency invests a great deal of energy into maintaining its 500 yards of white sand beach. In fact, the hotel's entrance has been designed so that visitors walking into the lobby can immediately see the beach. That view sets the pace for a resort where Hawaii's natural beauty is the dominant theme.

**LEFT:** Balconies, ceiling fans, and residential-style furniture reflect local design styles. **ABOVE:** Panoramic views encompass the pool, luxurious natural landscape, and the ocean beyond.

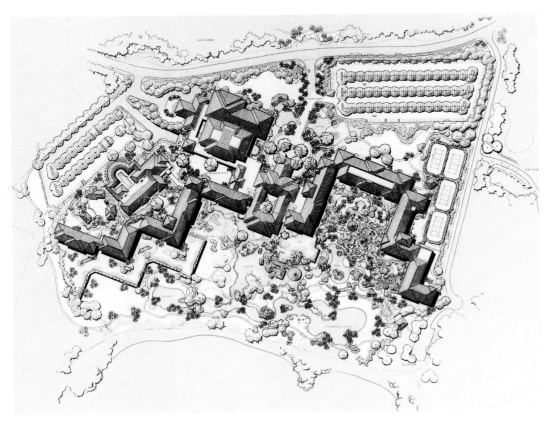

**HOTEL COMPANY**
THE SHILLA HOTEL COMPANY

**ARCHITECTS**
WIMBERLY ALLISON TONG & GOO
SAM WOO ARCHITECTS & ENGINEERS

**INTERIOR DESIGNER**
OGAWA FERRE-DUTHILLEUL
DECORATION

**PHOTOGRAPHER**
KYLE ROTHENBORG

ISLAND OF CHEJU, KOREA
# CHEJU SHILLA HOTEL

Southern California/Mediterranean-style architecture is not what

you expect to find at a Korean resort. And that is precisely the point

behind the Cheju Shilla, which was designed to draw local travelers

to a nearby destination that would seem exotic. But the hotel

succeeds, regardless of a visitor's cultural orientation, with

gorgeous indoor- and outdoor-swimming pools, a sprawling lobby,

light-filled interiors, and lushly landscaped grounds that are rich with

palm trees and local flora. Residing on an island with three

waterfalls, a coastline of spectacular basalt cliffs, and white sandy

beaches with unpolluted waters, the hotel's look blends seamlessly

with its surroundings.

The 330-room Cheju Shilla caters to a combination of tourists

and business travelers; the former are drawn to its bowling alley,

OPPOSITE ABOVE: A sweeping curve defines the sunbathing area.

OPPOSITE BELOW: The hotel's outdoor swimming pool is augmented with an ultrasonic whirlpool jacuzzi.

ABOVE: The design of the indoor pool elegantly departs from the hotel's Mediterranean aesthetic.

LEFT: The hotel's exterior recalls Southern California/Mediterranean architecture.

ocean-front recreation area, and extensive shopping, while the latter take advantage of the hotel's seven banquet and meeting rooms. All of the hotel's guest quarters feature extra-large bathrooms, subdued color schemes, soft lighting, and breathtaking views; also included are international direct dial telephones, 110/220 volt electric power, and private safe deposit boxes. Maintaining the Cheju Shilla's international aesthetic, its seven restaurants and lounges serve a variety of Korean, Japanese, and Western cuisines.

ABOVE: Duty-free shopping is made convenient at the Cheju Shilla's on-premises shop. LEFT: Vibrant floral motifs add colorful accents in the hotel's Royal Suite.

ABOVE: Shutters control light while adding a fresh look in a standard twin room. LEFT: The Presidential Suite combines traditional and contemporary elements.

## BANFF, CANADA<br>THE RIMROCK RESORT HOTEL

**HOTEL COMPANY**
THE RIMROCK RESORT HOTEL

**ARCHITECT**
COHOS, EVAMY, PARTNERS

**INTERIOR DESIGNER**
WILSON & ASSOCIATES

**PHOTOGRAPHER**
GARY CAMPBELL

Situated 700 picturesque feet above the town of Banff, The Rimrock is built into the side of Sulphur Mountain in the center of a popular ski resort. As would befit a hotel in this area, The Rimrock is casual yet elegant, with large, open public spaces and fabulous views from a seventh-floor lobby that is situated on the hotel's center landing. Green marble and sandy limestone augment a blue and green color scheme that plays off of the surrounding area's trees, sky, snow, and rock.

The hotel attracts many business travelers, though it also caters to a wide range of vacationers. Most of its 345 guest rooms and suites offer panoramic views of the breathtaking Bow River Valley, and some accommodations even come with balconies. Dark wood furniture and boldly colored fabrics dominate all of the rooms, which top out with a two-story presidential suite. Standing out from the hotel's relatively standard amenities are individual

OPPOSITE ABOVE: The hotel has been designed to unobtrusively blend in with its surroundings. OPPOSITE BELOW: Dark wood furniture dominates the hotel's public spaces. ABOVE: Decorated in a rustic style, a lobby sitting room looks out on the neighboring mountains. LEFT: As dusk descends, the hotel's lobby takes on a warm glow. RIGHT: The Rimrock is built into the side of Sulphur Mountain.

control systems in each room, which regulate the temperature via digital panels. Plus, unlike most neighboring hotels, The Rimrock's rooms have air-conditioning.

Attracting a large amount of convention business, the hotel offers a total of 16,000 square feet of meeting space. Boardrooms feature picture windows with mountain views, and state-of-the-art audiovisual equipment is available. The Rimrock's fitness center is equipped with a stone pool, massage facilities, squash courts, and weight-training equipment. Two restaurants and two cafes are on the premises for a variety of meals and snacks, all of them invariably enhanced by appetites worked up on the nearby slopes.

**ABOVE:** In an atmosphere of Mediterranean elegance, Ristorante Classico serves a wide range of Italian dishes. **LEFT:** A decorative chandelier enriches the ballroom's tailored ambience. **RIGHT:** The board rooms' beautiful views add a sense of magic to corporate meetings and presentations.

**ABOVE:** Rooms are decorated in bold colors that contrast with the earthy tones outside. **LEFT:** Many of the guest rooms provide balconies that offer breathtaking views.

**BELOW:** Sandy limestone is a predominant construction material at The Rimrock.

**HOTEL COMPANY**
HYATT HOTELS INTERNATIONAL

**ARCHITECT**
WIMBERLY ALLISON TONG & GOO

**INTERIOR DESIGNER**
HIRSCH BEDNER ASSOCIATES

**PHOTOGRAPHER**
JAIME ARDILES-ARCE

BALI, INDONESIA

# GRAND HYATT BALI

Some hotels try to be all things to all people, sublimating local design sensibilities to the point that they exude a single international style. Conversely, the Grand Hyatt Bali revels in the mystical sensibility that its location calls to mind. Further uniqueness stems from the hotel being split up into four different "villages." While each one exudes its own character, they all contain beautiful gardens, water motifs, and low-rise pagoda-type buildings. These characteristics combine to impart the facility with a strong sense of Balinese tradition.

The five-star resort hotel — constructed by as many as 10,000 workers at a time — spreads out over 60 landscaped acres and attracts travelers from around the world; not surprisingly, though, its traditional design holds particular appeal for visitors from the local region of Southeast Asia as well as Japan. Guest rooms are all decorated in a classic Balinese style, with wooden detailing,

OPPOSITE ABOVE: Garden pavilions serve as ideal locations for contemplating the beauty of Bali.

OPPOSITE BELOW: Breathtaking sunsets top off beautiful days at the Grand Hyatt Bali. LEFT: Expansive guest areas are made possible due to the hotel being situated on 60 acres of oceanfront property. BELOW: Pagoda-topped buildings and indigenous greenery surround the hotel's swimming pool.

locally crafted art, and traditionally curved furnishings. In addition to complete conference capabilities, the beachfront hotel offers a wide range of water-related activities and access to the Pacific Ocean. The emphasis on water is carried over to the landscape architecture, with rivers, falls, and cascading pools situated along the Grand Hyatt Bali's grounds.

Though the hotel features six different restaurants — serving a wide range of Asian and European cuisines — the most fitting meal can be enjoyed at Pesar Sengol. This is a buffet-style restaurant within a hotel-run marketplace, where diners are entertained by Balinese performers who dance on a built-in stage. Like nearly everything else in the hotel, it offers visitors a grand look at Bali's rich culture.

**LEFT:** Bamboo accessories appealingly impart the chain hotel with the feel of a locally run facility.

**BELOW:** The roofed but open-sided casual dining area is typical of Indonesian architecture.

**ABOVE:** Year-round outdoor dining ranks among the attractions at the Grand Hyatt Bali. **LEFT:** The hotel's Balinese water garden offers visitors a chance to enjoy a traditional dining experience. **BELOW:** Balinese statues greet visitors as they arrive for dinner.

RIGHT: The Balinese design aesthetic carries through to all of the hotel's guest rooms. BELOW: Gorgeous flowers bloom throughout the hotel's grounds. OPPOSITE: Balinese-style architecture has been employed throughout the hotel.

# LANAI, HAWAII
# THE MANELE BAY HOTEL

Backdropped by red lava cliffs and rock formations, The Manele Bay Hotel sits high above a white sand beach on Hawaii's sixth largest island. From each of the hotel's 250 guest rooms, visitors are afforded spectacular views of the ocean. Built in a traditional Hawaiian architectural style, The Manele Bay is housed in several two-story buildings that are surrounded by indigenous plants and dwarfed by towering palm trees.

The Manele Bay has been designed to provide seclusion and relaxation for a mix of business travelers and vacationers. Guests can enjoy picturesque rounds of golf on one of three nearby championship courses. Mornings on the links are often followed by relaxing strolls through the Hawaiian, Japanese, and Chinese gardens that are adorned with waterfalls, ponds, and streams. Guest rooms and suites are furnished in a simple, yet elegant manner, and many have balconies with spectacular views. The hotel's facilities include a health and fitness center, a library, nearby meeting facilities, and two restaurants that serve traditional Hawaiian fare and French Mediterranean cuisine. Snorkeling, diving, and hiking are all second to none at The Manele Bay Hotel.

**HOTEL COMPANY**
THE MANELE BAY HOTEL

**ARCHITECT**
ARNOLD SAVRANN

**PHOTOGRAPHERS**
MARY NICHOLS AND JEFFREY ASHER

ALL: The ocean-front Manele Bay affords comfortable accommodations with spectacular views. Hawaiian antiques and luxurious potted palms create an inviting ambience in the light filled Kailani Terrace. Six hand-painted murals by artist John Wullbrandt enhance the sitting area, an ideal setting for relaxing or socializing.

# ISTANBUL, TURKEY
# POLAT RENAISSANCE RESORT

The Polat Renaissance combines modern elegance with classic

Turkish design elements. Catering to international business

travelers as well as to tourists, the hotel boasts a lushly landscaped

rooftop swimming pool with a view of the Mamara Sea, a lively

**HOTEL COMPANY**
RENAISSANCE HOTELS

**ARCHITECT**
POLAT DESIGN GROUP

**INTERIOR DESIGNER**
DILEONARDO INTERNATIONAL

**PHOTOGRAPHER**
YAVNA ONAR

casino, and banquet/exhibit facilities. For those in need of

sustenance while gambling, there are dining tables situated among

the casino's roulette wheels and blackjack felts.

Throughout the hotel are six restaurants, including an eatery

that features gourmet Turkish seafood. Though their cuisines vary,

the restaurants share a Turkish/modern sensibility that runs

throughout the Polat. The stylish ambience carries over into all 400

rooms. Sophisticated and refined, they are dominated by four-

poster beds and wall-sized windows that let in plenty of light.

Carpets are earth toned and the walls are tastefully papered in a

striped pattern. The wood-framed furniture is invitingly reminiscent

of what you might find in a wealthy Turk's guest quarters.

**ABOVE:** The Polat Renaissance Resort shimmers against Istanbul's seaside sky. **LEFT:** The skylit lobby provides a comfortable area for guests to meet and greet visitors. **OPPOSITE:** A view of the Mamara Sea enhances a dip in the Polat's well-appointed, rooftop pool.

Fitness-minded visitors take advantage of the hotel's health club, and everyone seems to enjoy the comfortable atrium lobby. The Polat's overall aesthetic is epitomized by its lobby's mix of old and new: a marble-bordered, hammered-copper fountain resides alongside a fiber-optic sculpture that continually changes the ambience within the hotel space.

**ABOVE:** Classic Turkish furnishings and a full wine list combine to make in-room dining a memorable experience. **RIGHT:** The guest rooms are clubby and elegant, more reminiscent of what you would find in a private home than in the typical Turkish hotel.

TOP LEFT & RIGHT: Beyond the doors of the Casino Emperyal, a wide range of games awaits visitors who are eager to try their luck. BOTTOM LEFT: Some diners choose to enjoy their meals en casino. BOTTOM RIGHT: One of the Polat's half-dozen restaurants.

# THE RITZ-CARLTON, KAPALUA
MAUI, HAWAII

**HOTEL COMPANY**
THE RITZ-CARLTON HOTEL COMPANY

**ARCHITECT**
WIMBERLY ALLISON TONG & GOO

**INTERIOR DESIGNER**
FRANK NICHOLSON, INC.

**PHOTOGRAPHERS**
MICHAEL FRENCH, DONNA DAY AND
HOWARD J. WOLFF

Breathtaking views played a major role in the design of Kapalua's Ritz-Carlton. The rugged north Maui coastline can be seen from 80 percent of the hotel's 550 rooms, and the famous Kapalua Bay Golf Course is visible from the others. Taking advantage of surrounding sights, terraces at the hotel are plentiful and expansive. Additionally, major public spaces are outfitted with sliding glass panels that serve to bring the beauty of Maui's outdoors to the hotel's interior. Hotel corridors are lined with glass bifold doors that can be opened and closed quickly, thus accommodating the island's ever-changing climate.

The hotel caters to a mix of business and pleasure travelers who take advantage of its award-winning 54-hole golf course, 10,000-square-foot three-level swimming pool, 20 tennis courts, and a wide range of available water sports. There are six conference facilities that vary from a pair of 800-square-foot boardrooms to the 15,750-square-foot Ritz-Carlton Ballroom. The hotel's suites and guest rooms are all elegantly decorated with a European design sensibility and a fine selection of modern amenities. The hotel's six restaurants serve a variety of cuisines that range from traditional Hawaiian fare to Mediterranean dishes.

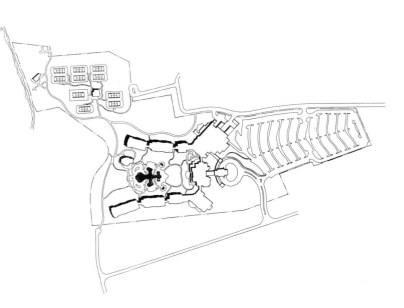

**OPPOSITE ABOVE:** Glass doors bring Hawaii's outdoors to the hotel's interior. **OPPOSITE BELOW:** Terraces abound at The Ritz-Carlton, Kapalua, allowing for beautiful views. **ABOVE:** Waterfalls add interest to the hotel's massive swimming pool. **RIGHT:** Suites at The Ritz-Carlton convey relaxed elegance.

HOTEL COMPANY
PENINSULA GROUP

ARCHITECT
THREE/ARCHITECTURE, INC.

INTERIOR DESIGNER
JAMES NORTHCUTT ASSOCIATES

PHOTOGRAPHER
JOHN VAUGHAN

## BEVERLY HILLS, CALIFORNIA
# THE PENINSULA BEVERLY HILLS

Understatement and elegance were obvious design goals in

creating the Peninsula Beverly Hills. In a town that is known for

showboating, this hotel remains unflinchingly cool and refined. Built

on the scale of a grand residence rather than a commercial facility,

it opens with an intimate entry foyer in lieu of the more traditional

large lobby. In fact, a sense of intimacy can be felt in all of the

hotel's smallish public spaces. Keeping with its simplistic design

philosophy, the Beverly Hills showplace has been adorned with few

antiques. However, what is there has been carefully chosen and is

of exquisite quality: 17th-century Italian embroideries, textiles from

China, and gorgeous French bronzes. In addition, a collection of

California Plein Air paintings from the 1920s and '30s are displayed

in the Peninsula's bar; this landscape-art motif continues through

the hotel, and all 196 guest rooms are decorated with commis-

sioned pieces from contemporary Plein Air painters.

**ABOVE:** City views unfold from a cabana-surrounded rooftop pool.
**LEFT:** The Peninsula's exterior exudes a look of old-world elegance.

**RIGHT:** The hotel is fronted by an intimate, understated foyer rather than a grand lobby. **BELOW:** Plush sofas and a lush view characterize the Peninsula's public spaces.

Rooms are traditional on the outside, but completely modern on the inside with fax machines, bedside control panels, and modem capabilities. Italian-style desks and extra-high cocktail tables can double as dining surfaces for room-service meals. The hotel is crowned by a rooftop pool and cabanas, an adjoining dining terrace that specializes in healthy cuisine, and a spa that features exercise rooms and a sauna.

**ABOVE:** Bathed in natural light, the ballroom is radiant, comfortable and elegant. **LEFT:** Eye-catching porcelain adorns the walls of the hotel's formal restaurant. **RIGHT:** The Peninsula's bar is decorated with California Plein Air paintings.

**LEFT:** Exercise facilities, steam rooms, and a sauna have been situated adjacent to the the rooftop pool. **BELOW:** Guest rooms have a traditional look, though they have been infused with high-tech capabilities.

HOTEL PRINCIPE FELIPE

FOUR SEASONS HOTEL LONDON

THE DALLAS MEDALLION

FOUR SEASONS HOTEL BOSTON

THE REGENT HONG KONG

FOUR SEASONS HOTEL LOS ANGELES

# REFURBISHED

# FOR THE '90s

**HOTEL COMPANY**
HOTEL PRINCIPE FELIPE, HYATT LA
MANGA CLUB RESORT

**ARCHITECT**
WIMBERLY ALLISON TONG & GOO
ASSOCIATES

**INTERIOR DESIGNER**
GREGORY AEBERHARD PLC.

**PHOTOGRAPHER**
ROBERT MILLER

HYATT LA MANGA CLUB RESORT, MURCIA, SPAIN

# HOTEL PRINCIPE FELIPE

Naming a hotel after its country's royalty sounds like a questionable

marketing ploy. However, in this particular instance the

endorsement was okayed by the Prince himself who is a frequent

guest in the newly renovated resort's Royal Suite. He joins an

international coterie of day-tripping golfers, leisure travelers,

families, and executives who enjoy being pampered while taking

care of business on the Spanish Mediterranean coast.

The five-star hotel's 192 rooms and seven suites are all

spacious, with oversized bathrooms, Spanish detailing, and cool,

Mediterranean elegance. Architects and designers collaborated to

outfit the resort with elements that would be redolent of the

location's predominantly Moorish heritage. The furniture, room

design, and hotel architecture were all created with a focus on local

color and homegrown materials.

In addition to convention facilities and a business center, the

Hotel Principe Felipe boasts Spike's Jazz Bar, a restaurant/club to

OPPOSITE ABOVE: Moorish arches define the porte-cochère. OPPOSITE BELOW: Fronting an 18-hole golf course, the Principe Felipe Hotel echoes Murcia's native architecture. ABOVE: The courtyard's wrought-iron balustrade, terracotta tile, light painted walls, and central fountain evoke the local landscape and architecture. LEFT: The lobby features metal pendants suspended from a vaulted ceiling, thus recreating the style of a grand old Spanish mansion.

which locals and visitors flock for music and tapas. Casual lunches
and formal dinners are available at Amapola, a versatile restaurant
where golfers refuel after rounds on the resort's 18-hole course.

**OPPOSITE:** The Hotel Principe
Felipe is an outgrowth of a 67-room
facility that initially served as little
more than an overnight accommoda-
tion for golfers. **ABOVE:** Suites are
roomy and comfortable, with art and
furnishings that echo the area's
Moorish roots. **LEFT:** Local manufacturers and artisans played large
roles in creating the furnishings for
each guest room.

ABOVE: Spike's Jazz Bar combines the look of a classic Spanish tapas bar with up-to-the-minute styling and technology. RIGHT: Leather, tapestries, sketches and copies of old masterpieces add warmth to the library.

LEFT: Rich wood paneling imbues the cocktail bar with a traditional look. ABOVE: The wrought-iron chandelier adds a Spanish design element in the ballroom. BELOW: The Amapola restaurant features special boxes in which golfers, fresh off the course, stash their cleats.

# FOUR SEASONS HOTEL LONDON

**HOTEL COMPANY**
FOUR SEASONS & REGENT HOTELS

**ARCHITECT**
MICHAEL ROSENAUER

**INTERIOR DESIGNERS**
TOM LEE AND ROSALIE WISE DESIGN

**PHOTOGRAPHERS**
JAN BALDWIN AND NIC BARLOW

Anyone who questions the elegance and discretion of the Four Seasons Hotel London need look no further than its guest register from 1972, the year that Howard Hughes laid low there for 11 months. These days the hotel caters primarily to less eccentric business travelers who are drawn to its large guest rooms, Park Lane address, and private garden. Detail oriented, the hotel has two-line phones and faxes, dual-voltage sockets, video players, and safes in every room. The popular Conservatory Bedrooms contain skylit, glass-walled sitting rooms that have been built onto their terraces.

Though the Four Seasons' 227 rooms are decorated in a classic British style — complete with chintz-covered sofas, wing back chairs, and Chippendale-style desks — the hotel maintains a modern aura. Its health club, which was added in response to guests' requests, has state-of-the-art equipment and even features television sets above each treadmill. Airy and light, the hotel makes extensive use of marble, and quality antiques are evident

OPPOSITE ABOVE: A terraced garden planted with ivy, hedges and flowering shrubs provides an added pleasure for hotel guests. OPPOSITE BELOW: London's Four Seasons Hotel towers over Hyde Park. ABOVE: Gleaming marble, fresh flowers and rich wood paneling set an elegant tone in the hotel's impressive lobby.

throughout. Management takes great pride in its five banquet/conference rooms, emphasizing that the spaces are flexible enough to serve as settings for social events, low-key board meetings, and theater-style conferences.

Though London is hardly known as a culinary capital, the Four Seasons places a strong emphasis on food. Hotel banqueting services can whip up everything from traditional British roasts to artistically designed platters of sushi. Besides offering guests three different restaurants to choose from, the Four Seasons Hotel London handles private dinners for parties of four to thirty-five in its refined sitting and dining rooms.

OPPOSITE: Fine food and an extensive wine list attract a mix of travelers and Londoners to the Four Seasons Restaurant. **ABOVE LEFT:** Harp music accompanies high tea in the Four Seasons' lounge. **ABOVE:** Lush greenery and a decorative scroll motif create visual interest behind the cocktail bar. **LEFT:** A mirror reflects restrained elegance in Lanes Restaurant.

ABOVE: A patterned wall covering and sheer window treatment maintain a subdued palette in the Wellington Suite. RIGHT: This double bathroom features an illuminated shaving mirror and its own speaker controls.

ABOVE LEFT: The Queen Anne Suite provides an intimate setting for business conferences. ABOVE: Chintz abounds in the hotel's Mayfair Suite. LEFT: Garden views and favorite TV shows are enjoyed by exercising guests at the Conservatory Fitness Club.

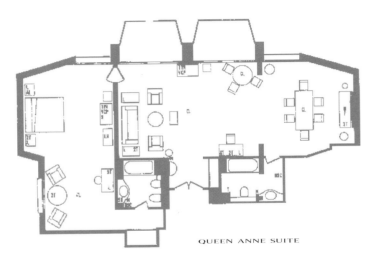

QUEEN ANNE SUITE

HOTEL COMPANY
MEDALLION HOTELS

ARCHITECT/INTERIOR
DESIGNER
BORDELON DESIGN ASSOCIATES

PHOTOGRAPHER
MICHAEL WILSON AND THE DALLAS
MEDALLION

## DALLAS, TEXAS
# THE DALLAS MEDALLION

Setting out to create Dallas's premier business hotel, the designers

of the Medallion realized that the project needed to be infused with

the same oversized sensibility that virtually defines Texas and the

New Hotel aesthetic. They did it by achieving the spirit of an open-

air park within the hotel, setting aside the lobby to serve as the hub

of activity. This effect is set off by a 10-story atrium highlighted by

a 12-foot waterfall and an eye-catching fountain. Sprawling, cleanly

designed in earth tones, and furnished with wooden pieces and

natural looking fabrics, the space is casual and inviting. Gazebo

palm trees, rattan chairs, and glass-topped cocktail tables supported

by logs conform with the park motif.

Catering primarily to business travelers, the 289-room

Medallion is the only hotel in North Dallas to provide 24-hour

concierge service. Guest rooms are casually designed in a style that

maintains the hotel's garden-house theme with rattan furniture,

flower-patterned pillows on the beds, and framed prints of palm

trees adorning the walls. Modern elements such as voice mail and

OPPOSITE ABOVE: The lobby lounge provides a casual area for relaxation. OPPOSITE BELOW: Rattan furniture and a garden motif define the hotel's lobby. ABOVE: Dallas can be viewed from the atrium's upper floors. LEFT: In the classic New Hotel style, the Medallion's Restaurant and Lounge are designed as open, airy spaces with areas for intimate conversation.

modem capabilities have been incorporated into each room's

infrastructure. The award-winning restaurant downstairs has an

open kitchen, serves new American cuisine, and is known locally

for its extensive wine list.

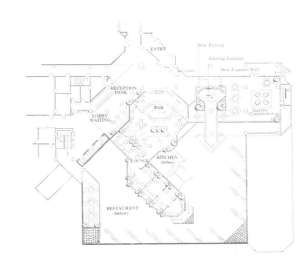

OPPOSITE: Towering palm trees soar 25 feet in the vast atrium.

ABOVE: The garden motif carries through to the hotel's guest rooms.

LEFT: The concierge lounge serves as an intimate public space.

**HOTEL COMPANY**
FOUR SEASONS & REGENT HOTELS

**ARCHITECT**
WZMH ASSOCIATES

**INTERIOR DESIGNER**
WILSON & ASSOCIATES

**PHOTOGRAPHER**
ROBERT MILLER

BOSTON, MASSACHUSETTS

# FOUR SEASONS HOTEL BOSTON

**ABOVE:** The hotel is nestled in the heart of Boston opposite the Public Garden. **BELOW:** The Bristol Lounge provides a casual environment for light meals and afternoon teas. **OPPOSITE:** The wood-paneled hotel lobby sets a tone of warmth and understated elegance.

A modest brick exterior belies the understated grandeur of the Four Seasons' interior. Located across the street from the Boston Public Garden and standing as New England's only recipient of the coveted AAA Five Diamond Award, the hotel is an attractive spot for business travelers. It boasts more than 13,000 square feet of meeting and function space and offers a Presidential Suite that is plush enough to truly live up to its name. Designed to resemble a ship captain's home, the suite is furnished with Chippendale reproductions and bonafide antiques. A mural of the Boston Harbor wraps around one of the dining room's walls, and a baby grand piano dominates the living room. For heads of state and heads of companies, it is a space that evokes status and taste.

Though the recently refurbished hotel's 287 other rooms appear more modest, they are all elegantly appointed and specifically turned out with business travelers in mind. There are three two-line phones in each room, modem capabilities have been built into the hotel's circuitry, some suites contain fax machines, computer rentals can be arranged, and secretarial services are available. The health club features a 40-foot lap pool, state-of-the-

art workout equipment, a sauna, and a whirlpool. The hotel's top restaurant, wood-paneled Aujourd'hui, offers award-winning contemporary American cuisine served in a warm, sophisticated setting that defines the entire hotel's ambience.

OPPOSITE: Relaxing alongside the hotel's 40-foot lap pool, guests can take in a view of the Boston Public Garden. RIGHT: Aujourd'hui, the hotel's award-winning fine dining room, is acclaimed for its contemporary American cuisine.

**ABOVE:** Executive Suites offer comfortable accommodations and conference areas. **ABOVE RIGHT:** Guest rooms are functional and refined. **RIGHT:** Guests feel pampered by the hotel's soft terry robes and generous supply of personal bath items.

**ABOVE:** The Presidential Suite is designed to resemble a ship captain's home. **RIGHT:** The hotel's simple brick facade belies its luxurious interiors.

**HOTEL COMPANY**
FOUR SEASONS & REGENT HOTELS

**ARCHITECT**
SKIDMORE, OWINGS & MERRILL

**INTERIOR DESIGNER**
CHHADA, SIEMBIEDA & ASSOCIATES

**PHOTOGRAPHER**
PETER SEAWARD

# KOWLOON, HONG KONG
# THE REGENT HONG KONG

Constructed along the border of Hong Kong's harbor, The Regent takes serious advantage of its location and views. Glass walls — reinforced to withstand waterfront winds of 180 kilometers per hour — encircle the hotel's upper floor, while a promenade down below allows guests to take picturesque strolls. Besides serving as a romantic spot for walking and dining, the promenade also operates as a buffer against typhoons and high swells during monsoon season. Hong Kong's first harbor-front highrise, The Regent is clad in marble rather than the less expensive and more common granite. Its lobby has been detailed in gleaming pink and black, creating an overall effect that is sleek and stunning.

The 602-room Regent, which was built in 1980, caters primarily to Western business travelers. In accommodating them, the hotel offers two banquet suites, nine harbor-view function rooms, two deluxe boardrooms, a smaller meeting room, and a comprehensive library; additionally, a wide range of business services are made available for guests. Once the work day winds down, corporate customers tend to find themselves particularly drawn to rooms that overlook the harbor through huge, tinted windows. Several suites have their own verandas, and two of the

**OPPOSITE ABOVE:** The lobby walls are made of extra-thick glass, allowing fantastic views while withstanding typhoon-season winds.

**OPPOSITE BELOW:** The Regent is Hong Kong's first waterfront highrise.

**ABOVE:** Yü seafood restaurant provides breathtaking views of Hong Kong. **LEFT:** Yü features a 44-by-7-foot curved aquarium bubble.

ABOVE: Glass doors enclose a private room at Plume, the hotel's premier restaurant. RIGHT: Meals at the luxurious Plume are frequently accented with selections from its 10,000-bottle wine cellar — the largest in Asia. BELOW RIGHT: Harbourside Restaurant offers informal dining in an alfresco setting.

poshest accommodations come equipped with private jacuzzis and terraced gardens. The hotel's four restaurants serve cuisines that range from Chinese, to continental, to prime USDA beef.

The Regent features marble bathrooms and deep tubs, an extensive art collection, and in-room furnishings characterized as "European designs of Ming Dynasty furniture." Beyond its guest quarters, the hotel offers a health spa with private rooms that contain saunas, steam showers, jacuzzi tubs, and solariums, where even the most stressed-out business travelers can unwind.

ABOVE: Expansive use of tinted plate glass affords panoramic views from rooms and suites. LEFT: Lounging poolside, guests enjoy stunning views across Hong Kong's harbor.

**HOTEL COMPANY**
FOUR SEASONS & REGENT HOTELS

**ARCHITECT**
GIN WONG ASSOCIATES

**INTERIOR DESIGNER**
MAYHEW DESIGN

**PHOTOGRAPHER**
JAIME ARDILES-ARCE

LOS ANGELES, CALIFORNIA

# FOUR SEASONS HOTEL LOS ANGELES

Residing on a palm-lined street near Beverly Hills, the Four Seasons offers rooms that provide unobstructed views of Hollywood, Bel-Air, and Century City. Its ground level is fringed with lush gardens of tropical foliage, and the hotel's public areas are highlighted by an impressive collection of European art. It is no wonder that this nine-year-old hotel has spent its existence serving as a favored lodging for film stars and show business executives.

The hotel's 285 rooms — 106 of which are suites — all come with step-out balconies that offer expansive views of Los Angeles. Guest rooms are decorated in a residential style, with floral, Oriental, and geometric details; the hotel's six Premier Suites and two Penthouse Suites all have individual, eclectic designs. Often doubling as on-the-road offices, the Four Seasons' accommodations feature multi-line telephones, fax/modem capabilities, voice mail, and packing/unpacking services. In addition to its Grand Ballroom,

**OPPOSITE ABOVE:** The Four
Seasons is located on an elegant,
palm-lined block near the Beverly
Hills border. **OPPOSITE BELOW:**
Even the smallest vestibules have
been meticulously furnished in a style
that is resolutely upscale. **ABOVE:**
Arriving by complimentary limousine,
guests find the hotel lobby to be elegant and inviting. **LEFT:** Power dining is convenient when a top restaurant is located just below a guest's
room.

the hotel offers 10 luxuriously appointed banqueting salons and an outdoor garden for informal meetings.

Situated on a beautifully landscaped terrace are outdoor pools, jacuzzis, and a tented exercise center; massage therapists and personal trainers are available upon request. Guests frequently take advantage of the hotel's five dining rooms, which serve a variety of California-inspired dishes.

**ABOVE:** Elegant detailing imparts this guest room with luxury and refinement. **RIGHT:** Private meals and banquets can be arranged through the hotel's kitchen. **BELOW:** The spacious Presidential Suite presents an eclectic mix of styles.

OPPOSITE: A canopied bed adds a sense of drama to the Presidential Suite. ABOVE: Swimmers enjoy a fabulous view of Los Angeles. LEFT: An outdoor terrace is one option for those who are dining at the hotel's Gardens Restaurant.

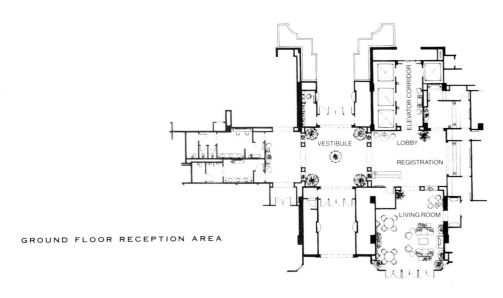

GROUND FLOOR RECEPTION AREA

VESTIBULE

LOBBY

ELEVATOR CORRIDOR

REGISTRATION

LIVING ROOM

THE PENINSULA HONG KON

BEVERLY HILLS HOTE

FOUR SEASONS HOTEL MILAN

THE RITZ-CARLTON SAN FRANCISC

THE ST. REGI

FOUR SEASONS RESORT SANTA BARBAR

HOTEL DE CRILLO,

THE PIERR

THE ORIENTAL, BANGKO

ESSEX HOUSE, HOTEL NIKKO NEW YOR

# CLASSICS

# RENEWED

# THE PENINSULA HONG KONG

One of the world's legendary grand hotels, Hong Kong's Peninsula

is an amalgam of state-of-the-art technology and time-honored

traditions. The service there recalls a more genteel era, the interior

design transports guests to the future, and its lavish lobby is a

throwback to glamorous times. A fleet of Rolls Royces is available

for chauffeuring guests to the airport or around the city, and a

**HOTEL COMPANY**
THE PENINSULA GROUP

**ARCHITECT**
ROCCO YIM PARTNERSHIP

**INTERIOR DESIGNER**
RICHMOND INTERNATIONAL

**PHOTOGRAPHER**
LAWRENCE YU

matching pair of helicopters are often employed for aerial tours of

Hong Kong. Everything at this 300-room hotel is designed to make

a statement: To swim in the rooftop pool is to enjoy a spectacular

view of Hong Kong's skyline; to enjoy a drink in the China Clipper

bar is to be immersed in a high-tech world of hard-edged chrome

and brushed metal. In other words, everything here is wonderfully

executed for maximum effect.

Catering primarily to business travelers, the hotel boasts a

business center that offers the most up-to-date international

**OPPOSITE ABOVE:** A throwback to glamorous days, The Peninsula's lobby shimmers as if it has been gilded. **OPPOSITE BELOW:** Conference rooms are sleekly designed with recessed ceilings and crystal chandeliers. **ABOVE LEFT:** A fleet of Rolls Royces is made available to hotel guests. **ABOVE RIGHT:** Shuttling by helicopter, time-pressed guests avoid traffic en route to the airport. **LEFT:** A legendary grand hotel, The Peninsula looms over one of Hong Kong's elite thoroughfares.

communications facilities available, as well as banquet and meeting rooms that are suitable for a wide range of functions. Eight bars and restaurants offer wonderfully broad combinations of food and ambience; they range from the elegant French cuisine of Gaddi's to the Euro-Asian dishes cooked at Felix, which is located on the roof and has been designed by cutting-edge architect Phillipe Starck. Considerably more subdued, guest rooms are decorated in a modern, yet comfortable combination of European and Oriental styles, and they offer stunning views of Victoria Harbour, Hong Kong Island, Kowloon, and the New Territories.

**ABOVE:** Twenty-first century design sets the pace for dining at Felix. **FAR LEFT:** Felix's Crazy Box, built from soft construction materials, offers a respite from the harder edged design aspects of the hotel. **LEFT:** Small, individually lit tables and a curved banquette create a feeling of intimacy with high-tech design elements.

**BELOW:** Careful lighting plays a major role in the look of Felix.

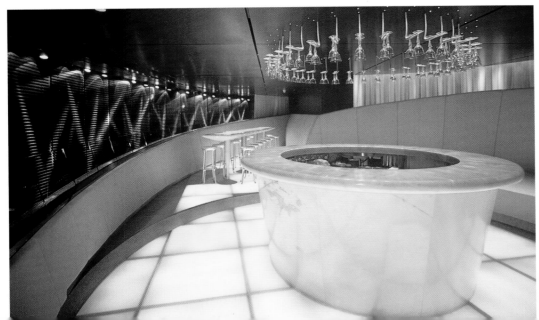

**RIGHT:** Eastern-style furnishings impart local elegance to private dining experiences at The Peninsula. **BELOW:** Relatively subdued in its design, Spring Moon offers traditional Chinese cuisine. **OPPOSITE TOP LEFT:** High-tech amenities are fitting accouterments in the China Clipper lounge. **OPPOSITE TOP RIGHT:** A combination of hard and soft construction elements gives an ultra-modern look to the China Clipper. **OPPOSITE BOTTOM LEFT:** The China Clipper's entrance is slickly designed and strategically lit. **OPPOSITE BOTTOM RIGHT:** Even in its restroom, the China Clipper's high-tech theme continues.

ABOVE: Marble bathrooms feature large tubs, double sinks, and harbor views. RIGHT: A combination of Western furnishings and Eastern design elements imparts guest rooms with a comfortable sense of place.

LEFT: A curved ceiling frames the view from this guest room. BELOW: Plush furnishings and a spacious balcony allow for comfort inside as well as out.

TOP: Soft lighting sets the mood in the hotel's spa. CENTER: Coolly realized curves contribute to the spa's relaxing aura. BOTTOM: Ornate columns add a Roman touch to the swimming pool.

**ABOVE:** On the Sun Terrace, even the umbrellas follow the hotel's streamlined aesthetic. **LEFT:** The Peninsula Spa is designed to make optimal use of natural light.

# BEVERLY HILLS, CALIFORNIA
# BEVERLY HILLS HOTEL

Deal making and the Beverly Hills Hotel's Polo Lounge have long gone hand in hand for players who have ranged from Howard Hughes to Alfred Hitchcock to Mike Ovitz. Now, with the hotel's three-year renovation complete, the recently reopened Polo Lounge is as hot a spot as ever. The same can be said for the rest of the facility as well. Operating since 1912, it was designed in that era's popular California mission style. Thirty years later, new buildings were constructed in the moderne style. The current renovation is an amalgam of both looks, combined with a freshly hatched Beverly Hills Hotel signature aesthetic: curved surfaces, plush custom carpets, and a banana palm motif that is evident in wall coverings, art work, and chandeliers.

The social center of the Beverly Hills community — ballrooms and wedding facilities are available there — the hotel attracts a heady mix of international travelers and Hollywood power

HOTEL COMPANY
BEVERLY HILLS HOTEL AND
BUNGALOWS

ARCHITECT
GENSLER ASSOCIATES

INTERIOR DESIGNER
HIRSCH BEDNER ASSOCIATES

PHOTOGRAPHER
ROBERT MILLER

**ABOVE:** At the Polo Lounge's power tables, some of Hollywood's biggest deals have been consummated.

**LEFT:** The hotel's ballroom looks out onto a lushly landscaped garden.

brokers. Fittingly, its 150 guest rooms and 25 bungalows come equipped with in-room fax machines and private phone lines. The latter offers the ultimate in discretion, allowing publicity-averting callers to circumvent the switchboard. The bungalows all have individual entrances, private jacuzzis, working fireplaces, and private patios. Lunch and breakfast are served in the Polo Lounge, where banquettes are the color of money; formal dinners that fuse European and California cuisines can be enjoyed in the Polo Grille, which is designed to be reminiscent of a luxury ocean liner; more casual meals are available in the hotel's Fountain Coffee Shop.

**ABOVE:** Banana palms are found throughout, even here, on the wall of a third-floor corridor. **LEFT:** With their elegant design, deluxe furnishings, and breathtaking views, even the hotel's standard rooms make guests feel like big-time players.

ABOVE: A calm but elegant ambience prevails in the bridal boudoir. LEFT: The design of this regular suite manages to be simultaneously luxurious and comfortable, helping to make the Beverly Hills Hotel a home away from home for countless film executives and frequent travelers. BELOW: The Presidential Suite's bathroom features marble walls and a private jacuzzi.

# MILAN, ITALY
# FOUR SEASONS HOTEL MILANO

**HOTEL COMPANY**
FOUR SEASONS & REGENT HOTELS

**INTERIOR DESIGNER**
BABEY • MOULTON, INC.

**PHOTOGRAPHER**
ROBERT MILLER

Those who worship at the altar of style will have an absolutely religious experience upon entering the Four Seasons' recently opened facility in the heart of Milan. Occupying what had once been a 14th-century convent, the hotel retains its soaring spires and massive columns, while the interior is a mélange of old, new, and ancient elements. Considering that Milan had long been surprisingly bereft of a top-flight hotel, regular business travelers to the city view this elegant outpost, where the concierge's desk is backed by a vintage fresco of the Three Wise Men, as nothing short of a blessing. Among Four Seasons Hotel Milano's better known guests are Donna Karan, Richard Avedon, and Ralph Lauren.

Because the hotel has only 98 rooms, it emotes the kind of intimacy that is usually experienced in a guest house. Ancient

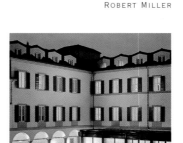

**ABOVE LEFT & LEFT:** A gorgeous courtyard is surrounded by a building that dates back to the 14th century. **ABOVE:** The structure's original columns have been left intact and in place in the hotel lobby.

LEFT: The hotel's most formal restaurant, Il Teatro, offers haute Italian cuisine. BELOW: La Terrace is a relaxed restaurant for fine dining.

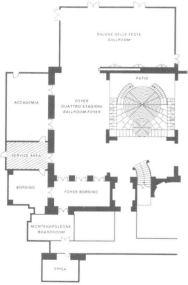

**ABOVE:** With heated floors and sunken tubs, guest bathrooms offer a sense of timeless elegance.

columns, arched walls, and vaulted ceilings dominate the lobby. Rooms vary in design and size, though the 28 suites and seven conference rooms are all decorated in soft styles, with light-colored custom fabrics and contemporary furnishings. Settings lean toward the neoclassical, with vaulted ceilings and restored fresco fragments. Modern touches include TV- and video-loaded armoires, two-line telephones, secretarial services, and one-hour garment pressing. The bathrooms are white marble masterpieces with deep soaking tubs, heated towel racks and floors, and non-steam mirrors. As would befit any grand hotel in Milan, the Four Seasons there offers 24-hour room service and three top restaurants that attract well-heeled local patrons as well as hotel guests.

ABOVE: In transforming the convent into a world-class hotel, care was taken to merge ancient details with modern touches. LEFT: Sleeping in the Ceiling Room is sure to bring on grandly themed dreams. BELOW: The bi-level suites each occupy three floors, and they are coveted for their high ceilings and private gardens.

HOTEL COMPANY
THE RITZ-CARLTON HOTEL COMPANY

ARCHITECT
WHISLER PATRI

INTERIOR DESIGNER
FRANK NICHOLSON

PHOTOGRAPHER
JOHN SUTTON

# SAN FRANCISCO, CALIFORNIA
# THE RITZ-CARLTON SAN FRANCISCO

Besides being an elegant addition to The Ritz-Carlton chain of hotels, the San Francisco branch actually doubles as a good civic deed. Before being christened with the famous lion-and-crown logo, this neoclassical Nob Hill building that now houses San Francisco's Ritz was entering its 10th year of neglect and deterioration. Rebuilt with inspiration from the site's original architectural drawings, the freshly glamorized, 336-room hotel opened in 1991 at a cost of $140 million. Expensive though the renovation may have been, it is also gloriously thoughtful: 75 percent of the building's window spandrels have been repaired and reused; and the lobby is a grand public space that's adorned with 18th-century antiques, illuminated by crystal chandeliers, and decorated with a museum-quality art collection.

The elegance carries over to guest accommodations. Besides their plush, residential-style sofas, tables, and chairs, the rooms all feature Italian marble bathrooms with double sinks, telephones, and separate water closets. Maid service is offered

OPPOSITE ABOVE: The neoclassical building that houses The Ritz-Carlton was constructed in 1909 as Metropolitan Life Insurance Company's Pacific Coast headquarters. OPPOSITE BELOW: Set on Nob Hill's eastern slope, The Ritz-Carlton is a regular stop on the California Street cable-car line. ABOVE LEFT: Crystal chandeliers and a world-class art collection add upscale sheen to the hotel's public spaces. ABOVE RIGHT: The Director's Room is decorated with rich, dark mahogany paneling. LEFT: Afternoon tea at The Ritz-Carlton, San Francisco is always an elegant affair.

twice daily, the hotel staff is multi-lingual, and child care is available.
Guests staying in The Ritz-Carlton Club — characterized as "the
hotel within the hotel" — receive continuous hors d'oeuvres and
cocktails, dedicated concierges, separate elevators for added
discretion, and access to two private conference suites. Additional
meeting facilities, occupying 400- to 9,500-square-feet, are available
along with state-of-the-art audiovisual equipment.

All guests can take advantage of the hotel's fitness center —
with steam rooms, a whirlpool, and full workout equipment —
three restaurants, and one cocktail lounge. The Dining Room, the
San Francisco Ritz's signature eatery, features a menu of critically
acclaimed, simply prepared dishes that can only be enhanced with
selections from its award-winning wine list.

**OPPOSITE:** The suites are large and formal enough for entertaining as well as sleeping. **ABOVE LEFT:** The Terrace Courtyard restaurant offers indoor and outdoor dining with a Cuisine Vitale menu that meets American Heart Association dietary guidelines. **ABOVE:** The indoor swimming pool is one facet of The Ritz-Carlton's extensive fitness center. **LEFT:** Decorated with hand-carved moldings and illuminated by Bohemian Crystal chandeliers, The Ballroom is an impressive setting for formal banquets.

# THE ST. REGIS
### NEW YORK, NEW YORK

**ABOVE:** The St. Regis's exterior is a fine example of Beaux Arts-style architecture. **BELOW:** The King Cole Bar, with its famous Maxfield Parrish mural, is where the Bloody Mary cocktail was created. **BELOW RIGHT:** The decor of Lespinasse rivals its food for sheer luxury. **OPPOSITE:** Cast in brass, diminutive chefs flank the French doors leading to Lespinasse, one of Manhattan's most acclaimed restaurants.

Open since 1904, The St. Regis has long ranked among Manhattan's most venerable luxury hotels. Now, following a four-year renovation, the hotel, fronted by a distinctive Beaux Arts-style facade, recoups its crown as one of the city's plushest spots for discerning business travelers and upscale tourists. Its marble and wood-paneled interiors have been restored in an exacting fashion, so as to retain turn-of-the-century elegance nearly 100 years after the fact. More pointedly, as Architectural Digest noted, the use of 22-karat gold leaf and marble from four different Italian quarries makes it hard to tell where thoughtful changes begin and longstanding traditions end.

In addition to its impressive grandeur, the 313-room hotel also boasts extraordinarily attentive service. There is a ratio of two staff members for every guest and a butler is stationed on each floor. Guest rooms are designed to meet high residential standards, complete with crystal chandeliers, marble baths, and custom-made

**HOTEL COMPANY**
ITT SHERATON

**ARCHITECT**
BRENNAN BEER GORMAN/ARCHITECTS

**INTERIOR DESIGNERS**
BRENNAN BEER GORMAN
MONK/INTERIORS
GRAHAM-KIM DESIGN

**PHOTOGRAPHY**
COURTESY OF THE ST. REGIS

wall and floor coverings. Bed linens are made from fine Egyptian cotton, china comes courtesy of Limoges, and Tiffany & Co. has designed the hotel's flatware. On a more high-tech note, rooms come with at least two telephone lines, a fax machine, computerized light and temperature controls, and state-of-the-art audio/video systems.

Besides housing the four-star restaurant Lespinasse, The St. Regis also boasts a clubby oak-paneled bar, a fashionable spot for afternoon tea, and 10 different function rooms. The latter accommodate parties of eight to five-hundred and are managed with the same gracious service and attention to detail that are the hallmark of the St. Regis.

ABOVE: A crystal chandelier helps to set the mood for gourmet in-suite dining. LEFT: The Christian Dior Suite's bedroom shows off the hotel's custom wall coverings and elegant furnishings.

**HOTEL COMPANY**
FOUR SEASONS & REGENT HOTELS

**ARCHITECT**
EDWARD PITTMAN ASSOCIATES

**INTERIOR DESIGNER**
JAMES NORTHCUTT ASSOCIATES

**PHOTOGRAPHER**
JAMES ARDILES-ARCE

SANTA BARBARA, CALIFORNIA

# FOUR SEASONS RESORT SANTA BARBARA

In renovating the Four Seasons Resort Santa Barbara, architect James Northcutt faced the challenge of updating and improving the hotel without hurting its well-entrenched sense of sophistication. He did it by enhancing original architect Reginald Johnson's classical detailing — including 1920s California interiors, dark-wood ceilings, and time-worn fixtures — as well as adding trompe l'oeil highlighting and top-quality antiques. The result is dramatic while remaining elegant, comfortable, and inviting.

That very feeling is evident in the hotel's furnishings. Pieces inspired by classic Italian and Portuguese designs play off of upholstered styles that are luxuriously alluring. Walls in the hotel are painted a soft peach, and the grounds have been lushly landscaped. Ocean views are capitalized on in public spaces, and interior lighting has been designed to create dramatic effects throughout the facility.

**OPPOSITE ABOVE:** Classic California architecture creates a feeling that is simultaneously elegant and comfortable. **OPPOSITE BELOW:** Many of the hotel's original architectural touches are evident in the newly renovated facility. **ABOVE:** Abundant natural light, rattan furnishings and distinctive floral arrangements create an inviting ambience. **LEFT:** Guest rooms are designed to be homey and comfortable. **RIGHT:** Carefully chosen, handpicked antiques are conspicuous throughout the hotel.

HOTEL COMPANY
CONCORDE HOTELS

ARCHITECT
JACQUES-ANGE GABRIEL

INTERIOR DESIGNER
SONIA RYKIEL

PHOTOGRAPHER
JOACHIM BONNEMAISON/AFFIRMATIF

# HOTEL DE CRILLON
### PARIS, FRANCE

ABOVE: Guests arriving at the hotel receive a warm and elegant reception in a room that dates back to the 18th century. BELOW: Hotel de Crillon affords breathtaking views of Place de la Concorde.

The ultimate testament to Hotel de Crillon, originally built in 1758 at the request of King Louis XV, is that one of its original rooms, complete with period wood panels, remains on permanent exhibit at New York's Metropolitan Museum of Art. Among those who have recently stayed at the hotel are I.M. Pei, Madonna, Michael Jackson, and chess wizard Gary Kasparov. It is decorated in a grand style, which leaves the Crillon looking more like a palace than a hotel.

Housing 163 rooms and suites, Hotel de Crillon recently underwent a renovation and redesign under the auspices of the French National Landmark Commission. The hands-on decorating was orchestrated by designer Sonia Rykiel. The most majestic examples of her work can be found in the magnificent Presidential Suites. Their chandelier-lit living rooms are dominated by baby grand pianos, gold-colored furniture upholstered in ruby red velvets, and trompe l'oeil ceilings. Other rooms and suites contain classical terraces, Corinthian columns, and Versailles-style parquet floors; decorational items include Aubusson carpets, Bohemian crystals, and oversized, gold-leaf Wedgwood chinas.

A pair of superb restaurants — L'Obelisque, the less formal of

ABOVE: Exquisite 18th-century tapestries provide a timeless backdrop for modern technology. TOP RIGHT: A decorative balustrade and panoramic view enhance the Leonard Bernstein terrace. ABOVE RIGHT: Fashion designer Sonia Rykiel has redecorated the hotel's suites with richly colored, classically designed furnishings. RIGHT: A Baccarat masterpiece of gilded brass and crystal graces the hotel's salon.

the two, is a fashionable hot spot of the moment — a tea salon, and a bar are all ideally elegant places for guests who need to entertain or simply refuel.

HOTEL COMPANY
FOUR SEASONS & REGENT HOTELS

ARCHITECT
SCHULTZE AND WERNER

PHOTOGRAPHER
JAMIE ARDILES-ARCE

# NEW YORK, NEW YORK
# THE PIERRE

The recipient of a $75-million renovation in 1992, The Pierre remains a touchstone to a gentler, more civilized era. Beyond its ornate decor, mansard roof, and manually operated elevators, the hotel offers a level of personalized service that is rarely found anywhere these days. Guests can arrange for in-room shopping through Manhattan's top department stores and boutiques, room service may be ordered around the clock, and one-hour pressing is available for unexpectedly wrinkled garments.

Catering primarily to international business travelers, The Pierre's staff is multi-lingual, speaking a total of 28 languages. All 202 guest rooms have safes, two-line phones, and fax/modem capabilities. Decorated in The Pierre's signature blue-and-white color scheme, they feature plush chairs, mahogany armoires, and oversized bathtubs. Guests staying in the hotel's Grand Suites luxuriate with panoramic views of Central Park, preferred amenities of their choice, and Frette linens.

Public areas at the hotel include a half-dozen meeting spaces and ballrooms, chic Cafe Pierre, a state-of-the-art fitness center, and the ornately muraled Rotunda with its trompe l'oeil ceiling.

ABOVE: The landmark hotel occupies one of Manhattan's most coveted blocks of real estate. BELOW: Ornate molding and gilt detailing imbue the lobby with luxury and elegance.

LEFT: Multiple television sets and a hand-painted mural prevent boredom in the hotel's 1,600-square-foot workout facility. BELOW: Afternoon tea in the opulent Rotunda is a Manhattan tradition.

# THE ORIENTAL, BANGKOK

Founded in 1876, The Oriental, Bangkok, originally served as its namesake city's only high-quality hotel. Today it stands among many luxury hostels there, though The Oriental clearly remains one of Bangkok's plushest. Located on the River Wing, the 396-room hotel has been built in an architectural style that is traditionally Thai in appearance. Its room interiors are classic and luxurious, outfitted with four-poster beds, hardwood floors, satellite television, and telephones that have direct international calling capabilities. The style, elegance, and amenities offered by The Oriental are lush enough to have pleased celebrated guests such as Joseph Conrad, Gore Vidal, and John Le Carre.

Much of what draws elegant patrons, who stay at The Oriental on business as well as pleasure trips, are the hotel's many facilities and services. The pampering begins when guests land at the airport and can arrange to be shuttled across the River Wing on one of the Oriental's jet-propelled, air-conditioned boats. Once arriving, after checking in, corporate guests take advantage of eight international restaurants, six function rooms, and a business center that provides translation and secretarial services as well as fax and

**HOTEL COMPANY**
THE ORIENTAL, BANGKOK

**PHOTOGRAPHER**
R. IAN LLOYD

OPPOSITE ABOVE LEFT: The lobby combines ancient and modern design elements. OPPOSITE ABOVE RIGHT: Air-conditioned river boats transport guests from the hotel to the mainland. OPPOSITE BELOW: Viewed at dusk, The Oriental shimmers like a jewel. LEFT: Dark woods add a touch of natural elegance to the hotel's interior. ABOVE: Bangkok's finest French restaurant, The Normandy, offers spectacular views and impeccable service. BELOW LEFT: The Oriental Spa offers opportunities for meditation and relaxation.

**LEFT:** The Somerset Maugham Author's Suite is decorated in an elegant, traditional Thai style. **BELOW:** Four-poster beds and classic Thai elegance emanate from the hotel's finest rooms.

telex access. Pleasure travelers choose from a wide range of activities and diversions, including a Thai Cooking School and Culture program at which they learn the local ways of dining and living; the Sports Center, which features a high-tech gym, squash courts, and a sauna; and the hotel's unique Oriental Spa with its herbal remedies that do wonders for jet lag.

ABOVE: Named after the American
pulp novelist, the Jim Thompson Suite
is more luxurious than any of the settings conveyed in his writing. LEFT:
Hardwood floors and four-poster beds
are signatures of The Oriental,
Bangkok's style.

HOTEL COMPANY
ESSEX HOUSE, HOTEL NIKKO
NEW YORK

ARCHITECT AND
INTERIOR DESIGNER
PIERRE YVES ROCHON

PHOTOGRAPHY
COURTESY OF ESSEX HOUSE

# NEW YORK, NEW YORK
# ESSEX HOUSE, HOTEL NIKKO NEW YORK

When the Essex House opened its doors in 1931, the art deco enterprise had been designed to be the tallest, largest hotel in Manhattan. There were 1,286 rooms and some of the most magnificent views in town. The Central Park views are still there, but following a 1991 renovation, the hotel has reduced its accommodations to 595 guest rooms and 77 suites, all more spacious than the original architects had envisioned. They are also far more modern with connections for computers and fax machines, dual-line telephones, and individual temperature controls. The rooms' Louis XVI- and Chippendale-style furnishings, however, retain their timeless elegance.

Catering primarily to business travelers, the hotel makes a point of offering a wide range of business services and equipment. Essex House's Business Center is outfitted with fax and teletype machines, Macintosh and IBM computers, a Japanese word processor, a business library, and dictation equipment; business personnel for hire include secretaries, translators, and staff members who can expedite the processing of photographic transparencies. There are six function rooms, two board rooms, and the availability of many audiovisual aids.

ABOVE: The hotel's facade is a classic example of stylized 1930s architecture. BELOW: Essex House's lobby recalls the hotel's art deco heritage.

TOP LEFT: Journey's Bar exudes the aura of a traditional men's club. TOP RIGHT: Les Celebrites, Essex House's premier restaurant, received three stars from The New York Times. BOTTOM LEFT: A blend of traditional and contemporary elements creates restrained elegance in the Presidential Salon. BOTTOM RIGHT: Tailored formality reigns in the Presidential Suite's spacious bathroom.

# DIRECTORY

## HOTELS

**BEVERLY HILLS HOTEL**
9641 Sunset Boulevard
Beverly Hills, California 90210
United States
Tel: (310) 276-2251
Fax: (310) 887-2887

**CHEJU SHILLA HOTEL**
3039-3 Saekdal-Dong
Seogwipo, Island of Cheju
South Korea
Tel: (064) 38-4466
Fax: (02) 230-3587

**THE DALLAS MEDALLION**
4099 Valley View Lane
Dallas, Texas 75244
United States
Tel: (214) 358-9000
Fax: (214) 788-1174

**ESSEX HOUSE, HOTEL NIKKO
NEW YORK**
160 Central Park South
New York, New York 10019
United States
Tel: (212) 247-0300
Fax: (212) 315-1839

**FOUR SEASONS HOTEL BOSTON**
200 Boylston Street
Boston, Massachusetts 02116
United States
Tel: (617) 338-4400
Fax: (617) 351-2251

**FOUR SEASONS HOTEL LONDON**
Hamilton Place, Park Lane
London W1A 1AZ
England
Tel: 171 499 0888
Fax: 171 493 6629/1895

**FOUR SEASONS HOTEL LOS ANGELES**
300 South Doheny Drive
Los Angeles, California 90048
United States
Tel: (310) 273-2222
Fax: (310) 859-3824

**FOUR SEASONS HOTEL MILANO**
Via Gesu, 8
Milan 20121
Italy
Tel: 2-77088
Fax: 2-7708-5000

**FOUR SEASONS HOTEL NEW YORK**
57 East 57th Street
New York, New York 10022
United States
Tel: (212) 758-5700
Fax: (212) 758-5711

**FOUR SEASONS HOTEL SINGAPORE**
190 Orchard Boulevard
Singapore, 1024
Tel: (65) 734-1110
Fax: (65) 733-0682

**FOUR SEASONS RESORT
SANTA BARBARA**
1260 Channel Drive
Santa Barbara, California 93108
United States
Tel: (805) 969-2261
Fax: (805) 969-4682

**GRAND HYATT BALI**
P.O. Box 53,
On Nusa Dua Beach
Nusa Dua, Bali
Indonesia
Tel: 361-771-234
Fax: 361-772-038

**GRAND HYATT JAKARTA**
Jalan M.H. Thamrin
P.O. Box 4546
Jakarta
Indonesia 10045
Tel: 61-21-390-1234
Fax: 61-21-334-321

**HOTEL DE CRILLON**
10 Place de la Concorde
Paris 75 008
France
Tel: 44 71 15 00
Fax: 44 71 15 02

**HOTEL INTER-CONTINENTAL
LOS ANGELES**
251 S. Olive Street
Los Angeles, California 90012
United States
Tel: (213) 617-3300
Fax: (213) 617-3399

**HOTEL PRINCIPE FELIPE,**
Hyatt La Manga Club Resort
Los Belones
30385 Cartagena, Murcia
Spain
Tel: 34 137234
Fax: 34 68564603

**HOTEL SOFITEL BUCHAREST**
Boulevard De L'Exposition No 2
Sector 1
Bucharest
Romania
Tel: (401) 223-40 00
Fax: (401) 222 46 50

**HYATT REGENCY ISTANBUL**
Taskisla Caddesi 80090
Taksim, Istanbul
Turkey
Tel: 90212-225-7000
Fax: 90212-225-7007

**HYATT REGENCY KAUAI**
1571 Poipu Road
Koloa, Island of Kauai
Hawaii
United States
Tel: (808) 742-6226
Fax: (808) 742-6229

**HYATT REGENCY OSAKA**
1-13-11 Nanko-Kita, Suminoe-Ku
Osaka 559
Japan
Tel: (81) (6) 612-1234
Fax: (81) (6) 614-7800

**THE MANELE BAY HOTEL**
P.O. Box 310
Lanai City, Island of Maui
Hawaii 96763
United States
Tel: (808) 565-2397
Fax: (808) 565-2032

**MANILA DIAMOND HOTEL**
Roxas Boulevard, Corner Drive,
J. Quintos Street
Malate, Manila
Philippines
Tel: 632-536-2211
Fax: 632-536-0392

**THE ORIENTAL, BANGKOK**
48 Oriental Avenue
Bangkok 10500
Thailand
Tel: (66-2) 236 0400
Fax: (66-2) 236 1937

**PARK HYATT SYDNEY**
Hickson Road, The Rocks, 2000
Sydney
Australia
Tel: 61-2-241-1234
Fax: 61-2-256-1555

**THE PENINSULA BEVERLY HILLS**
9882 Santa Monica Boulevard
Beverly Hills, California 90212
United States
Tel: (310) 273-4888
Fax: (310) 858-6663

**THE PENINSULA HONG KONG**
Salisbury Road
Kowloon
Hong Kong
Tel: (852) 2366 6251
Fax: (852) 2315 3213

**THE PIERRE**
2 East 61st Street
New York, New York 10021
United States
Tel: (212) 838-8000
Fax: (212) 826-0319

**POLAT RENAISSANCE RESORT**
Manolya Sokak No. 25
Istanbul
Turkey
Tel: 011-90-1-268-7133
Fax: 011-90-1-264-9938

**THE REGENT HONG KONG**
18 Salisbury Road
Tsim Sha Tsui
Kowloon
Hong Kong
Tel: 2721 1211
Fax: 2739 4546

**RIHGA ROYAL HOTEL NEW YORK**
151 West 54th Street
New York, New York 10019
United States
Tel: (212) 307-5000
Fax: (212) 765-6530

**THE RIMROCK RESORT HOTEL**
P.O. Box 1110
Mountain Avenue
Banff, AB
Canada TOL OCO
Tel: 403-762-3356
Fax: 403-762-1842

**THE RITZ-CARLTON, KAPALUA**
One Ritz-Carlton Drive
Kapalua, Island of Maui
Hawaii
United States
Tel: (808) 669-6200
Fax: (808) 669-3908

**THE RITZ-CARLTON SAN FRANCISCO**
600 Stockton Street
San Francisco, California 94108-2305
United States
Tel: (415) 296-7465
Fax: (415) 291-8559

**THE ROYAL ABJAR HOTEL**
P.O. Box 8668
Dubai
United Arab Emirates
Tel: 971-4-62555
Fax: 971-4-697358

**ROYAL PARK HOTEL NIKKO**
2-2-1-3 Minato Mirai
Nishi-ku, Yokohama
Japan
Tel: 045-224-5060
Fax: 045-224-5165

SHUTTERS ON THE BEACH
One Pico Boulevard
Santa Monica, California 90405
United States
Tel: (310) 458-0030
Fax: (310) 458-4589

STOUFFER CONCOURSE HOTEL
One Hartsfield Centre Parkway
Atlanta, Georgia 30354
United States
Tel: (404) 209-9999
Fax: (404) 209-8934

THE ST. REGIS
Two East 55th Street
New York, New York 10022
United States
Tel: (212) 753-4500
Fax: (212) 541-4736

THE WESTIN HOTEL
One West Exchange Street
Providence, Rhode Island 02903
United States
Tel: (401) 598-8000
Fax: (401) 598-8200

## ARCHITECTS & DESIGNERS

ANCHOR MORTLOCK &
WOOLLEY PTY., LTD.
180 Goulburn Street
Sydney, NSW2010
Australia
Tel: (612) 264-5366
Fax: (612) 283-2969

BABEY • MOULTON, INC.
633 Battery Street
San Francisco, California 94111
United States
Tel/Fax: (415) 394-9910

BIRCH COFFEY DESIGN ASSOCIATES
206 East 63rd Street
New York, New York 10021
United States
Tel: (212) 371-0100
Fax: (212) 371-0104

BORDELON DESIGN ASSOCIATES
675 Bering Drive, Suite 875
Houston, Texas 77057
United States
Tel: (713) 789- 9681
Fax: (713) 789-4387

BRENNAN BEER GORMAN/ARCHITECTS
515 Madison Avenue
New York, New York 10022
United States
Tel: (212) 888-7667
Fax: (212) 935-3868

BRENNAN BEER GORMAN
MONK/INTERIORS
515 Madison Avenue
New York, New York 10022
United States
Tel: (212) 888-7667
Fax: (212) 935-3868

CHHADA, SIEMBIEDA &
ASSOCIATES LTD.
2nd Floor, Wilson House Ltd.
19-23 Wydam Street
Hong Kong
Tel: 2521-2191
Fax: 2810-6061

CHHADA, SIEMBIEDA & PARTNERS
400 Oceangate, Suite 1100
Long Beach, California 90802
United States
Tel: (310) 437-5444
Fax: (310) 437-2452

COBOS, EVAMY, PARTNERS
200, 902-11 Avenue SW
Calgary, AB T2R OE7
Canada
Tel: 403-245-5501
Fax: 403-229-0509

DESIGN CONTINUUM, INC.
5 Piedmont Center, Suite 300
Atlanta, Georgia 30305
United States
Tel: (404) 266-0095
Fax: (404) 266-8252

DILEONARDO INTERNATIONAL
2350 Post Road
Warwick, Rhode Island 02886
United States
Tel: (401) 732-2900
Fax: (401) 732-5315

PAUL DRAPER AND ASSOCIATES, INC.
4106 Swiss Avenue
Dallas, Texas 75206
United States
Tel: (214) 824-8352
Fax: (214) 824-0932

FLATOW, MOORE, BRYAN,
SHAFFER & MCCABE
809 Copper Avenue, NW
Albuquerque, New Mexico 87102
United States
Tel: (505) 766-6610
Fax: (505) 764-9861

THE FRASER NAG PARTNERS
P.O. Box 1775
Dubai
United Arab Emirates
Tel: 971-4-22-0222
Fax: 971-4-22-6105

GENSLER ASSOCIATES
2500 Broadway, Suite 300
Santa Monica, California 90404
United States
Tel: (310) 449-5600
Fax: (310) 449-5850

GRAHAM-KIM DESIGN
282 Montvale Avenue
Woburn, Massachusetts, 01801-4697
United States
Tel: (617) 935-3444
Fax: (617) 935-3894

GREGORY AEBERHARD PLC.
Berkshire House
168-173 High Holborn
London WC1V7AA
England
Tel: 171 465 8855
Fax: 171 465 8856

K. HARA ASSOCIATED ARCHITECTS
AND ENGINEERS
New Ginza Daiichi Building, 7-11-10
Ginza, Chuoku, Tokyo 104
Japan
Tel: 8133-574-6251
Fax: 8133-572-6894

HILL ARCHITECTS
The Stanford Barn, 700 Welch Road
Palo Alto, California 94304
United States
Tel: (415) 617-0366
Fax: (415) 617-0373

HIRSCH BEDNER ASSOCIATES
3216 Nebraska Avenue
Santa Monica, California 90401
United States
Tel: (310) 829-9087
Fax: (310) 453-1182

HIRSCH BEDNER ASSOCIATES
4/F Kai Tak Commercial Building
317-321 Des Voeux Road Central
Hong Kong
Tel: 8522-545-2051
Fax: 8522-542-2022

HOK INTERNATIONAL ASIA
PACIFIC LTD.
Unit 2403-6 Shui on Centre
6-8 Harbour Road
Hong Kong
Tel: 852-2824-1903
Fax: 852-2824-1874

IMAGE DESIGN
1300 Parkwood Circle, Suite 450
Atlanta, Georgia 30339
United States
Tel: (770) 952-7171
Fax: (770) 933-9093

INTER ART ETUDES
70 rue Michel Ange
75016 Paris
France
Tel: 1 46 51 42 71
Fax: 1 46 51 16 23

MAYHEW DESIGN
705 North Alfred Street
Los Angeles, California 90069
United States
Tel: (213) 655-0737
Fax: (213) 655-7719

THE NICHOLS PARTNERSHIP
2600 Douglas Road, Suite 900
Coral Gables, Florida 33134
United States
Tel: (305) 443-5206
Fax: (305) 446-2872

FRANK NICHOLSON, INC.
360 Massachusetts Avenue
Acton, Massachusetts 01720
United States
Tel: (508) 369-0900
Fax: (508) 369-1138

JAMES NORTHCUTT ASSOCIATES
717 N. La Cienega Boulevard
Los Angeles, California 90069
United States
Tel: (310) 659-8595
Fax: (310) 659-7120

OBAYASHI CORPORATION
Design Studio #1
4-33 Katahama-Higashi
Chuo-Ku Osaka
Japan 540
Tel: 816-6139201
Fax: 816-6139256

OGAWA FERRE-DUTHILLEUL
DECORATION
33 Rue Saint-Augustin
75002 Paris
France
Tel: 1 47 42 90 20
Fax: 1 47 42 03 86

WHISLER PATRI
2 Bryant Street
San Francisco, California 94105
United States
Tel: (415) 957-0200

PEI COBB FREED AND PARTNERS
600 Madison Avenue
New York, New York 10022
United States
Tel: (212) 751-3122
Fax: (212) 872-5443

EDWARD PITMAN ASSOCIATES
120 East La Guera
Santa Barbara, California 93101
United States
Tel: (805) 963-0845
Fax: (805) 966-6454

PIERRE YVES ROCHON
12, Avenue Matignon
75008 Paris
France
Tel: 1 44 95 84 84
Fax: 144 95 84 70

SONIA RYKIEL
175, Boulevard Saint Germain
75006 Paris
France
Tel: 1 49 54 60 00
Fax: 1 49 54 60 96

SAA PARTNERSHIP
78 Shenton Way, No. 24-00
Singapore 0207
Tel: (65) 220-0411
Fax: (65) 224-9929

ARNOLD SAVRANN
Castle & Cook Properties, Inc.
P.O. Box 2780
Honolulu, Hawaii 96803
United States
Tel: (808) 548-4811

SKIDMORE, OWINGS & MERRILL
333 Bush Street, Suite 2200
San Francisco, California 94104
United States
Tel: (415) 981-1555
Fax: (415) 398-3241

STUBBINS ASSOCIATES
1033 Massachusetts Avenue
Cambridge, Massachusetts 02138
United States
Tel: (617) 491-6450
Fax: (617) 491-710

THOMPSON VENTULETT STAINBACH &
ASSOCIATES, INC.
12th Floor North
CNN Center
Atlanta, Georgia 30303-2705
United States
Tel: (404) 888-6600
Fax: (404) 888-6700

THREE/ARCHITECTURE, INC.
3624 Oak Lawn, Suite 111
Dallas, Texas 75219
United States
Tel: (214) 559-4080
Fax: (214) 559-0990

CARL TRIMBLE ARCHITECTS
1210 Spring Street NW
Atlanta, Georgia 30309
United States
Tel: (404) 874-6161

WEIDELPLAN
Maybachstrasse 33
D-7000 Stuttgart 30
Germany
Tel: 49711-8107-0

FRANK WILLIAMS & ASSOCIATES
154 West 57th Street
New York, New York 10019
United States
Tel: (212) 582-4685
Fax: (212) 974—5471

WILSON & ASSOCIATES
3811 Turtle Creek Boulevard,
15th Floor
Dallas, Texas 75219
United States
Tel: (214) 521-6753
Fax: (214) 521-0207

WILSON & ASSOCIATES
8811 Alden Drive, Suite 12
Los Angeles, California 90048
United States
Tel: (310) 275-6551

WIMBERLY ALLISON TONG & GOO
2222 Kalakaua Avenue, Penthouse
Honolulu, Hawaii 96815
United States
Tel: (808) 922-1253
Fax: (808) 931-1692

WIMBERLY ALLISON TONG & GOO
2260 University Drive
Newport Beach, California 92660
United States
Tel: (714) 574-8500
Fax: (714) 574-8550

WIMBERLY ALLISON TONG
& GOO ASSOCIATES
Waldon House, 2nd Floor
57 Old Church Street
London SW35BS
England
Tel: 171 376 3260
Fax: 171 376 3193

GIN WONG ASSOCIATES
9346 Santa Monica Boulevard
Beverly Hills, California 90210-3604
United States
Tel: (310) 550-1800

SAM WOO ARCHITECTS & ENGINEERS
137-070 Han Wom Building
1449-12 Seocho-dong
Seocho-ku, Seoul
South Korea
Tel: (02) 521-4100
Fax: (02) 521-7131

ROCCO YIM PARTNERSHIP
2034 Harbour Center
#17 Kennedy Road
Hong Kong
Tel: (852) 2528 0128
Fax: (852) 2529 2135

# PHOTOGRAPHERS

JAIME ARDILES-ARCE
730 Fifth Avenue
New York, New York 10019
United States
Tel: (212) 333-8779
Fax: (212) 593-2070

JAN BALDWIN
11 Gibralter Walk
London E2 7LH
England
Tel: 171 935 2626
Fax: 171 935 7557

NIC BARLOW
Nic Barlow Photography
40 Holland Park
London W113RP
England
Tel: 171 229 3600
Fax: 171 460 0441

JOACHIM BONNEMAISON
AFFIRMATIF
18 rue de Miromesnil
75 008 Paris
France
Tel: (1) 42 65 40 91

GARY CAMPBELL
1316 1st Street SW
Calgary, AB T2R OV7
Canada
Tel: 403-233-2575
Fax: 403-234-7473

MICHAEL FRENCH
P.O. Box 360218
Dallas, Texas 75336
United States
Tel/Fax: (903) 432-4893

ALAIN GOUSTARD
Images de la ville
3, avenue Adolphe Schneldor
92140 CIAMART
Paris
France
Tel: (1) 46 38 36 28
Fax: (1) 46 38 22 62

WARREN JAGGER
150 Chestnut Street
Providence, Rhode Island 02903
United States
Tel: (401) 351-7366
Fax: (401) 421-7567

OLIVIER KONING
Wimberly Allison Tong & Goo
2222 Kalakaua Avenue, Penthouse
Honolulu, Hawaii 96815
United States
Tel: (808) 922-1253
Fax: (808) 931-1692

ROB MCGREGOR
Perspective Images
20-22 Parsons Avenue
Springvale 3171
Australia
Tel: 03 95585367
Fax: 03 95585025

ROBERT MILLER
10929 Howland Drive
Reston, Virginia 22091
United States
Tel/Fax: (703) 758-9818

MILROY & MCALEER
711 W. 17th Street, #G7
Costa Mesa, California 92627
United States
Tel: (714) 722-6402
Fax: (714) 722-6371

PETER PAIGE ASSOCIATES
269 Parkside Road
Harrington Park, New Jersey 07640
United States
Tel: (201) 767-3150
Fax: (201) 767-9263

KYLE ROTHENBORG
Rothenborg Pacific
2559 Ipulei Way
Honolulu, Hawaii 96816
United States
Tel: (808) 523-1000

PETER SEAWARD
c/o Leo Burnett
6/FL, Cityplaza 3
14 Taikoo Wan Road
Hong Kong
Tel: 2884 6411
Fax: 2885 3209

JOHN SUTTON
8 Main Street
Point San Quentin, California 94964
United States
Tel: (415) 258-8100

PETER VITALE
P.O. Box 10128
Santa Fe, New Mexico 10128
United States
Tel: (505) 988-2558
Fax: (505) 982-6412

MICHAEL WILSON
Michael Wilson Photography
7015 San Mateo Boulevard
Dallas, Texas 75223
United States
Tel/Fax: (214) 328-8627

HOWARD J. WOLFF
Wimberly Allison Tong & Goo
2222 Kalakaua Avenue, Penthouse
Honolulu, Hawaii 96815
United States
Tel: (808) 922-1253
Fax: (808) 931-1692

LAWRENCE YU
Lawrence Studio Photography
Flat E, 3/F, Po Ming Building
Foo Ming Street, Causeway Bay
Hong Kong
Tel: (852) 2890 9231
Fax: (852) 2891 9235

# INDEX